Praise for

Blind Hope

"With humorous and poignant asides, Meeder beautifully bridges the gap between the sad and silly, showing the lovely and forsaken aspects of the individual heart so powerfully that readers will be coaxed into revisiting their understanding of the rescue God readily offers to all."

—PUBLISHERS WEEKLY

"*Blind Hope* is a powerful story, made even more beautiful by the fact that it is not simply a fairy tale. Kim Meeder creatively recalls for us how Laurie Sacher's unique interactions with the dog she saved ended up pointing her back to her Savior. In a culture obsessed with reality TV, I pray our hearts can not only be entertained and perhaps touched by this true story, but that we would be changed by it."

—ANGELA ALCORN STUMP, co-author of *The Ishbane Conspiracy*

"On her ranch in Oregon, Kim Meeder brings wounded horses and broken kids together and sees healing miracles on a regular basis. *Blind Hope*, a wonderful analogy of how God sees and loves his children, shows how a blind and ill dog named Mia helped to bring healing, love, and acceptance to the young woman who rescued her. Laurie's statement 'My dog is blind…

and now I see' is the story of all of us. This book could change your life."

—LAURAINE SNELLING, author of *No Distance Too Far*, all the Red River series, and *One Perfect Day* along with many other novels

"I thank God for Kim Meeder—she is one of my heroes! Her passionate love for the Lord, for children of all ages, and for animals is inspiring. She is thoroughly dedicated to whatever assignment God brings her way, including writing this beautiful account of the special bond between a woman and her dog. Kim brings an ongoing message of hope with this story, and she does it so well."

—DANAE DOBSON, author of *Let's Walk the Talk*

"Skidboot opened my eyes to a lot of life and love. After reading about Laurie and Mia, I learned even deeper lessons that our four-legged friends can teach us. This book shows very clearly how God has used dogs to spread his love. Thank you, Kim and Laurie, for sharing this story."

—DAVID HARTWIG, friend of Skidboot, the world-famous Texas blue heeler, featured in *Angel Dogs with a Mission: Divine Messengers in Service to All Life*

"Kim Meeder takes the reader along on a unforgettable journey with Laurie and her blind dog, Mia. Dog and human bring out the best in each other through hardship and friendship as the bond between the two grows deeper. And the beauty of nature provides the path that Laurie and Mia travel as they experience the ups and downs during teachable moments."

—JOAN DALTON, founder and executive director, Project POOCH

"Kim Meeder again shares a touching story of how God continues to use all of creation to move in and through our lives. *Blind Hope* gives us another glimpse into the amazing animal-human bonds that can bring fullness to our lives and move us to reach out to others, to reach out to hope, joy, and authentic love."

—DANNA L. HARVEY, animal-assisted therapy handler

"Poignant and convicting. I was touched by the way Kim told Laurie and Mia's story. I hope I can be as open to hearing the voice of God through unexpected ways."

—DIANE BLOYD KENT, volunteer for Guide Dogs for the Blind

"The human-animal bond is a special connection. Kim Meeder highlights this in *Blind Hope* as she draws parallels between each one of us and our Savior, Jesus Christ. As Kim says, 'To trust, listen, and believe takes time and practice.' She surely knows how to portray an important message of salvation while entertaining and showing life lessons with Laurie and Mia."

—ROXIE MUDDER, volunteer for Guide Dogs for the Blind

Praise for Kim Meeder's Previous Books

"Kim Meeder vibrantly shares—and lives—an amazing story of hope and restoration. A triumph of recovery for wounded hearts."

> —LOUIE GIGLIO, director, Passion Conferences,
> best-selling author

"I love good stories, and these are among the very best. Kim Meeder writes with a mesmerizing, wonderfully refreshing beauty. If your soul needs a fresh touch, reading this book is like opening a door and welcoming hope inside."

> —ALICE GRAY, best-selling compiler of *Stories for the Heart*

BLIND HOPE

Other Books by Kim Meeder

Hope Rising
Bridge Called Hope

BLIND HOPE

An Unwanted Dog &
the Woman She Rescued

KIM MEEDER
and LAURIE SACHER

MULTNOMAH
BOOKS

BLIND HOPE
PUBLISHED BY MULTNOMAH BOOKS
12265 Oracle Boulevard, Suite 200
Colorado Springs, Colorado 80921

Details in some anecdotes and stories have been changed to protect the identities of the
persons involved.

ISBN 978-1-60142-280-4
ISBN 978-1-60142-281-1 (electronic)

Copyright © 2010 by Kim Meeder and Laurie Sacher
Photography © 2010 by Benjamin Edwards

Published in association with the literary agency of Alive Communications Inc., 7680
Goddard Street, Suite 200, Colorado Springs, CO 80920, www.alivecommunications.com.

Published in the United States by WaterBrook Multnomah, an imprint of the Crown
Publishing Group, a division of Random House Inc., New York.

MULTNOMAH and its mountain colophon are registered trademarks of Random House Inc.

Library of Congress Cataloging-in-Publication Data
Meeder, Kim.
   Blind hope : an unwanted dog and the woman she rescued / Kim Meeder and Laurie
Sacher.—1st ed.
      p. cm.
   ISBN 978-1-60142-280-4 — 978-1-60142-281-1 (electronic)
   Includes bibliographical references.
   1. Sacher, Laurie. 2. Christian biography—Oregon. 3. Human-animal relationships—
Religious aspects—Christianity. 4. Dog owners—Religious life. 5. Dogs—Religious
aspects—Christianity. I. Sacher, Laurie. II. Title.
   BR1725.S15M44 2010
   277.3'083092—dc22
   [B]

                                             2010009799

Printed in the United States of America
2011

10 9 8 7 6

—〰—

For Laurie

Thank you for your courage in choosing to be transparent and honest. In doing so, you knew you would become vulnerable to the judgment of others. Yet you took that risk on the chance that through your story…some would find hope.

This little book has become that endeavor; it is your Blind Hope.

Contents

The Humble Beginning

Dear friend,

Before you come along on this journey with a woman, a friend, and a dog, please allow me to take you back to the founding of the ranch, the single seed from which this story was gleaned. Just like I tell our visitors, I would say to you now, "This is how it all began. Come, walk with me…

"At first, there was nothing…nothing except a hole in the ground."

—⁓—

Crystal Peaks Youth Ranch arose from extremely humble beginnings. In 1995 my husband, Troy, and I purchased the only piece of property we could afford—a forlorn, abandoned rock quarry that had been mined for cinders. The local department of transportation crushed this abrasive stone to spread across winter roads for traction. The property looked as if a hungry giant had unceremoniously chomped out a three-acre bite from the upper half. The massive wound inflicted by the mining operation had also removed all the trees, grass, and topsoil. What remained was nothing more than a gaping red hole in the ground.

Completely devoid of its former natural beauty, the land looked so hideous that no one else wanted it. One fact others overlooked was the pit's location on the western side of a small mountain. In Central Oregon, that means the acreage possessed a panoramic view of the Cascade Range, part of the Pacific Ring of Fire. This mountain range divides the entire state of Oregon with a row of formidable volcanoes ranging in elevation from seven thousand to more than eleven thousand feet. From the rim of the cinder pit, this parade of more than a dozen towering peaks creates a majestic skyline.

Looking outward at this geological masterpiece was awe inspiring. In contrast, looking downward was mortifying. Thankfully, in this life we each get to choose in which direction we will cast our gaze. We each get to decide where our focus will reside.

Troy and I chose to focus on what we could do. We chose to concentrate on the view and to restore a severely wounded piece of property.

Together, we appealed to the owners of the neighboring ranches for their garbage. The following two years, shovelful by shovelful, we hauled anything organic to cover the floor of our pit in order to create a seedbed. To renew the land, we brought in hundreds of tons of used stall shavings, moldy hay, and manure and spread them across the rocky wasteland that had become our residence. Troy, who at that time was a landscape contractor, carted home damaged and unwanted trees. Armed with shovels, picks, and pry bars, we dug large holes in which to plant the homeless trees. We often worked late into the night, with the vast, open darkness illuminated only by the headlights of our truck.

It was during this time that our first rescued horses arrived. I had been volunteering at a local breeding ranch, where I saw such atrocities that I would often leave vowing under my breath, "Someday this needs to change; someone needs to do something." I believe everyone faces a time when that "someday" is today and that "someone"…is you.

Everyone faces a time when that "someday" is today and that "someone"… is you.

I knew those devastated creatures wouldn't survive much longer, so I negotiated their release. Of the two, one was a gray Anglo-Arab, emaciated to the point of missing about three hundred pounds, a third of her normal body weight. Denied the nourishment to grow properly, she had a chest so narrow that I couldn't fit my closed fist between her front legs.

The second mare was a tall red bay with enormous brown eyes. I had witnessed the owner attack this lanky Anglo-Arab in such a savage rage that afterward he had to call a vet to come and suture a six-inch gash on her face.

Unknown to us at that time, those two rescued souls would become the forerunners of a vast stampede of needy horses soon to follow.

Troy and I watched in complete amazement as our ravaged property, filled with broken trees and broken horses, was transformed into the perfect setting to heal the hearts of broken children.

Drawn by word of mouth, kids started coming to the ranch—kids we didn't even know. Typically a friend of a friend had told them about these formerly abused horses that needed help. The children would walk up our driveway armed with little more than the desire to offer their unique brands of love. Remarkably, the kids weren't coming for what they could get but for what they could give.

At that time, our horses weren't trained, nor were they strong enough to carry a rider. So the kids helped in all aspects of their care. Some children only wanted to groom the horses, taking extra time to comb, condition, and braid their manes and tails. Others stood with great patience, holding up large rubber pans of specialized feed to help the horses regain their lost weight. Many kids simply wanted to lead the mares up the grassy hill and just sit and watch them graze.

Feeding carrots to the horses ranked as a favorite fun activity. Brilliant orange foam lined each horse's mouth as it chewed surplus loads of carrots. The horses savored the moment with heads down and eyes half closed, drooling pools of pure enjoyment. The sight and sound of that event always generated giggles from the children.

We watched in awe as these young ones—in their efforts to make the horses better—became better themselves.

Of all the kids who came to the ranch, there was one teenage girl who captured my heart. She was so broken inside that she had retreated into a world of silence. Although she could speak, she chose not to. Over time, I saw her reason for coming to the ranch: to feel safe and loved. Despite my efforts to release this young woman from her wordless prison, I was firmly locked out.

One day I was summoned away from her to take a long-distance phone call. When my call ended, I looked out the window and down the hill to check on her. She had taken the starving horse out and tied her to the hitching rail, and I could see their heads, lowered and close together. Curious, I kept watching. Finally the girl's head bobbed up, along with the horse's. And then I could clearly see what was happening. She was talking to the horse! From a starving girl to a starving horse, years of words poured out that no one had ever heard. From their parallel lives of pain, each understood the other better than most could understand either one of them. That was the moment when I knew I needed to build a place for this miracle of healing to thrive.

Simple encouragement from the little ranch in a cinder pit is reaching around the world.

Inspired by that singular occurrence of wondrous freedom, we decided to take action, and Crystal Peaks Youth Ranch was born. I determined to build a ranch where this type of release could happen without hindrance. A place that would come to be known as "The Ranch of Rescued Dreams."

Since those early days, we've seen the ranch grow into an international phenomenon. Our twice-yearly Information Clinics have helped bring more than one hundred similar ranches into existence across the United States, Canada, and abroad. Simple encouragement from the little ranch in a cinder pit is reaching around the world. Since 1995 we've been involved in the rescue of more than three hundred horses and have welcomed approximately five thousand visitors during our annual season from March to Thanksgiving. To date, an estimated fifty thousand have been served by this tiny ranch—all free of charge.

The ranch continues to exist because of the generosity of others. With thirty resident horses and a paid staff, Crystal Peaks maintains its ability to reach out to horses, children, and families in need because of those who believe in our program and do what they can to support it.

One method of provision for Crystal Peaks is our long-term volunteer program, ranging from two to eight months. Working with our volunteers for an extended time gives us the opportunity to know their hearts. How they respond to others during times of physical and emotional stress is of particular significance. When the need arises to hire someone new, we look first to this group of volunteers.

Laurie Sacher came to our ranch through the volunteer program and is now a member of our staff. Her desire to give, to make a difference here in this place, compelled her to travel north from her home in the foothills of northern California. Equipped with a minimal knowledge of horses and a wish to work with kids, Laurie came to Crystal Peaks with a heart eager to serve.

This book tells the story of Laurie and a dog, with some un-likely rescues along the way. I hope you enjoy the journey, my friend.

God Bless.

K

Kim Meeder

Prologue

The Sound of Trust

I t was seventeen degrees. Earth, snow, and sky converged into a milky emissary, whispering a timeless message of hushed peace. It was January in Central Oregon, and a glorious ice fog had coated every blade and branch with a one-inch layer of spiny rime. The frozen filigree embellished everything with its delicate crystal creations. Muted light shrouded all living things, now held captive in the icy embrace. The silent landscape murmured the promise of deep, abiding rest.

For me that rest would have to wait. I turned my truck off the dirt road that stretches north of Tumalo Reservoir and parked in the snow. From this access point, a wide wilderness invites adventurers to explore its latticed tangle of forgotten logging roads. I stowed my keys in a zippered pocket in my black running jacket and pulled on a pair of stretchy gloves. Soon my friend would meet me here for a long Sunday afternoon jog. Laurie and I were training for a marathon, her first and my tenth.

From the cab of my truck, I reveled in the peaceful setting. Weary from a heavy week of work, my heart welcomed the refuge of quiet. The small hiatus of silence soon was invaded, however, by the growing excitement of my dog, a Queensland blue heeler. She whined in anticipation, willing me to open the truck door to one of her favorite activities: a run in the snow with her mom.

Like all true ranchers, I never go anywhere without my faithful dog. Seven, or Sevi for short, is my third hand and foot and the thinking half of my brain. I'm sure she would finish my sentences if she could talk—and do a much better job of it! Dogs that live with us—really live with us—often know their human friends better than we know ourselves.

Dogs that live with us— really live with us—often know their human friends better than we know ourselves.

The comfort of my truck's heater subsided, and brittle barbs of frigid air prickled through the glass. I snuggled my hat down over my ears and zipped up my jacket under my chin.

When I stepped out of the truck, cold air engulfed me like an unseen wave. With my first quick breaths, I inhaled what felt like a million needles of ice. The assault on my throat and lungs drove me to hoist my collar even higher to cover my mouth.

While waiting for Laurie, I followed my prerun regimen, gearing up to spend a few hours in significant cold. I alternated jogging in place with pogo jumps to remain loose and warm. Sevi jumped around me in ecstatic leaps. Her chorus of happy yips beckoned me, as if to say, "Hurry up! We have a wonderful world to explore!"

In matters of life, dogs just get it. Sevi has taught me volumes more than I could ever hope to teach her. When it comes to demonstrating qualities like respect, forgiveness, and obedience and expressing emotions like love, joy, and peace, my dog operates on a level I can only hope to attain. Few creatures know how to maximize the moment better than a dog.

Few creatures know how to maximize the moment better than a dog.

Sevi's example constantly reminds me that ten minutes ago is already in the past, so why think about the future when right now is just so much fun? Her exuberance for life shows me how to really enjoy the rich and simple pleasures found within each moment of my days.

Sevi and I persisted in our frigid dance until Laurie arrived. Her white car was almost invisible against the pallid backdrop of the wintry High Desert. After a quick hug, Laurie and I agreed on our time frame and what trail to explore. The breath from our brief conversation froze into thin veils, drifting above us like drowsy angels. Not wishing to stiffen in the deep cold, Laurie retrieved her dog, Mia, and the four of us set off.

Sevi and Mia collided in a jubilant canine hug and then bounded up the trail ahead of Laurie and me. Our once relaxed breath now rose behind us in measured white puffs. Shoulder to shoulder, like twin steam engines, we chugged over a crunchy mantle of frozen snow. Every stride took us deeper into a pristine realm of winter wilderness.

One metered breath at a time, our voices soon merged with the serene environment. Like a smooth stone skipping across a mirrored pond, our dialogue bounced from one subject to another. After several miles, I noticed something else between Laurie's words. Because the rhythm of her voice had maintained a steady flow, I hadn't been aware of it earlier. It wasn't until Mia missed the turnoff onto a narrow, frozen logging road that I heard it—Laurie's voice calling her straying dog back to her side.

All during our run, Laurie had been guiding Mia with voice commands that barely punctuated our conversation. Laurie achieves this weaving of dialogue and instruction with such intrinsic skill I had all but forgotten that she does it for one reason: Mia is almost completely blind.

It wasn't until Mia bolted in the opposite direction that Laurie finally stopped and backtracked, calling out to her wayward friend. Unsure of how to help, I watched as Mia crashed through the frozen brush. She clambered over logs and tripped in a dense tangle of underbrush. Finally, overwhelmed by an icy prison she couldn't see, Mia stopped. A tinge of concern crept into my heart as Mia began to move again, turning in tight circles. She swung her head back and forth in an effort to locate her master. Laurie waded into the wintry snarl and broke through to where Mia was trapped. With gentle hands, Laurie turned her blind dog back in the direction of the correct path, and together they started out again.

I could hear Laurie's low voice guiding her courageous dog. "Easy, easy...step up, that's it. Here...here. Good girl." In unison they crunched up the trail toward me.

Laurie and I often run together, but I still admired their interaction as they trotted up to rejoin Sevi and me. Laurie resumed our run and conversation as if nothing more than a comma had passed between us since our last words.

Mia fell in right behind us, following the sound of our feet drumming over the frozen layer of earth and snow. I doubted that any onlooker would have been able to detect that Mia is blind. By tucking in at Laurie's heels, Mia relaxed behind a shield of protection she could sense but not see.

As long as Mia stayed close enough to hear Laurie's muted commands—and obeyed them—she was able to navigate an unknown world. Yet the moment Mia stopped listening to her master and chose instead to wander, everything changed. Once Mia was separated from Laurie, her world quickly compressed into a dangerous and lonely place.

Mia was following the sound of her master's footsteps. Her previous experiences had taught her that this was a sound she could trust. A sound that kept her safe.

The moment Mia stopped listening to her master and chose instead to wander, everything changed.

I smiled at Laurie and pointed a gloved thumb over my shoulder at her dog. My words were measured out between breaths. "What faith… to follow a master…you cannot see."

1

The Rescue

When Laurie arrived at the ranch, one of my first impressions of her was that she was tall—taller than me. Barefoot, I stand at five feet nine inches; in work boots I'm closer to six feet. Although I admire and respect many of my female peers, it isn't that common for me to literally look up at them. Nonetheless, before me stood a young woman of athletic stature crowned by sandy hair. Her sapphire eyes were framed by long, dusky lashes that neither needed nor were adorned with mascara. I would later come to know what lay beneath her exterior—a heart full of struggle, compassion, and sensitivity.

Laurie's summer season as a volunteer at Crystal Peaks ended with a new beginning. She was hired on as a permanent part of our family, our staff. Like everyone else, she wrestled with her intrinsic weaknesses, but she also had kindness, tenacity, and a great capacity to try. One year linked arms with another, each drawing our lives together more closely than the last. The tall, lovely girl that had breezed up my hill had also walked into my heart and turned into a friend.

Part of my job, and my joy, is spending one-on-one time with my staff members on the ranch. My intention for these meetings, while varying in its delivery, is to provide individual encouragement, challenge, and mentoring. Even though I'm thought to be the leader, I'm usually the one who emerges from those times of transparency feeling as if I've been mentored.

One of those transparent moments occurred when Laurie and I hiked around "the block." The block is an old dirt road that meanders in a lazy four-mile loop around our ranch. Rather than sitting in an office chair, I much prefer my real place of work, the great outdoors. Often it is while striding around in this fresh setting that lives are changed—including mine.

Laurie and I were heavily bundled, our knit caps pulled down low. Random snowflakes wandered down from the low gray sky. I waited for Laurie to lead the conversation, and she didn't disappoint.

"Well, you already know about the dog I rescued a while

back. For the last few months I've been giving you updates of what Mia and I are learning together. But I've never had the chance to really tell you how it all started and why this little dog means so much to me."

Her last words were wrapped in emotion.

Many voiceless steps trailed out in the velvety snow behind us. Laurie's silence spoke to me of her determination to contain her emotions. Finally, my friend's fragile resolve dissipated like the frozen breath that drifted over her shoulder. I heard a sob and turned to look at her.

Tears had gathered on her lower lashes and shimmered momentarily before sliding down her cheeks. I reached over and placed a gloved hand between Laurie's shoulders to bridge the small distance between us and peered into her glistening eyes. A single bare finger emerged from layers of long sleeves and gently pressed beneath her nose.

She took a deep breath. "When I rescued my dog, she was a discarded, homely mutt. I will never forget my first thought when I saw her: *She's a wretched creature…just like me.*"

Next, my friend poured out the story of how she had become the unlikely owner of a most unlikely dog.

No one could have foreseen then the significance of that day, least of all Laurie.

—⚮—

Her dog's rescue occurred on a blistering afternoon in late August. The day was devoid of the cooling breath that routinely moves across the High Desert. Scorching air hung still and silent, as if creation itself had given up hope and stopped breathing altogether. Even by Central Oregon standards, it was hot, miserably hot. The combination of searing heat and roadside sage produced an aroma so pungent that it could almost be tasted.

The stifling heat didn't deter Laurie. She was on her way, determined to prove to those around her that she was as kind and generous as anyone else who worked at the ranch. On this special day, she was going to rescue an unwanted dog.

She's a wretched creature…just like me.

The week before, Laurie had learned through our ranch office of a rescue situation with a horse and several dogs in need of new homes. This information was familiar to a rescue facility, but somehow this situation seemed different to Laurie in a way she couldn't define. Her residence wasn't conducive to rescuing a horse, but she could welcome a dog in need. Laurie wasn't able to shake off her persistent desire to help, and like her ranch co-workers, she decided to extend herself to a dog trapped in hardship.

One hopeful thought led to another. This could be the very thing that would lift her aching soul and carry her toward the shore of lasting contentment. Perpetually stalked by low self-esteem, Laurie clung with fresh hope to this adoption. She anticipated how this noble deed would help her feel better about herself. All she wanted was a hideaway, a reprieve from the relentless guilt of past poor decisions that continued to splinter her soul. Maybe this new horizon of selflessness would finally bring relief. Laurie's emotions soared with each thought, and she chose to soar with them.

Only days before, she learned the dog that was soon to be hers was an Australian shepherd mix about nine years of age. Laurie imagined a beautiful tricolored Aussie with piercing blue eyes. Further indulging her daydream, the new owner pictured this cool dog as her new sidekick, joining her in every hike, jog, and horseback ride. Her knowledge that Aussies are energetic, intelligent, and social only added to the framework upon which Laurie was building her dream.

Laurie's expectations multiplied as she traveled the twisting road to where the dog awaited. She envisioned walking with her silky-coated dog through the trendy downtown streets of Bend, Oregon. Dogs and their owners are so welcome in this hip scene that many merchants provide watering bowls outdoors and dispense dog biscuits indoors. Laurie pictured herself with her stylish dog at her side and smiled in advance approval, knowing the two of them would fit right in.

With her hopes as high as the afternoon's temperature, Laurie turned her car into the dilapidated yard that matched the given address. In an instant she knew why the call regarding the animals residing here had come to the ranch. The family lived in an old mobile home that was in the obvious process of returning to the crumbling earth beneath it. Everything appeared to be dead: the trees, the grass, and all the scattered, rusting cars.

A lone horse stood motionless near the sagging barbed wire fence that encircled it. Laurie breathed a heavy sigh and reminded herself that the underweight gelding would be moved later in the day to the new adoptive home found for him by the ranch. Goats and chickens, dogs and children, dotted the ramshackle landscape. Laurie's heart ached for them all.

Laurie made her way up wobbly wooden stairs and knocked lightly on the door, triggering a barrage of barking from within. The door opened a few inches, and a stocky woman peeked out. After brief introductions, the owner ducked back inside and then returned, leading the dog Laurie had promised to adopt. Laurie's earlier excitement fell like a blazing meteor.

This dog doesn't look anything like the dog I had imagined!

The dog was almost completely white with a brown patch

over each eye and a single brown spot on her rump. Her coat was a dull, tangled mess. Despite the intense heat, the Aussie's underbelly, from chin to tail, was shrouded with a three-inch swath of stinking guard hair. The dog was so thin she looked to be half her normal body weight.

Laurie's heart recoiled.

What? You've got to be kidding me! This isn't the dog for me. She's not nice looking at all! There has to be some mistake; this can't be my dog! Why did I say yes to a dog I'd never seen? What was I thinking?

Suddenly Laurie felt too ashamed of her shallow motives to admit out loud that, based solely on how the dog looked, she didn't want to take her. Yet if she declined to take the dog after seeing her, everyone would know that her loving compassion was only a facade; she would be exposed as a fake. Laurie rubbed her hand across her mouth in an attempt to hide her deepening disappointment. She stifled a moan of frustration, all the while hating herself in the awkward moments of silence.

Why did I say yes to a dog I'd never seen?

When the dog saw Laurie appraising her, she lowered her head and began to wag the entire back half of her body in a plea to be accepted. Laurie heard a strained "Hi, baby" drift off her lips as she knelt down to greet the wiggling dog. The canine's breath greeted her first—it was horrible! She fought to keep from reeling backward. The owner stood nearby and watched. While the dog licked her entire face, Laurie struggled to control her gag reflex, and her expression matched that of a woman being slapped repeatedly in the head with a giant putrid slug. Laurie pulled away just in time to see the dog's rotten teeth smiling at her.

This just keeps getting better and better, she thought, jerking her nose away from the stench that puffed from the dog's mouth. Standing back up, Laurie could do little more than stare at this homely dog with the ugly coat, bad breath, and nasty teeth.

Attacked by a dual ambush, Laurie fought to suppress the negative emotions inside her heart and the negative thoughts inside her head.

Get a grip! Even though this isn't the dog I pictured—the dog I wanted—I want even more to do the right thing. This dog cannot stay here; she won't survive. I can take her home and help her stabilize by regaining the weight she has lost. If I must, I can find a suitable home for her then. I simply cannot leave her here—not now, not after seeing her plight. Today—right now—she needs my help. And I'm not leaving without her!

Laurie squared her shoulders and looked over at the owner. "I'll take her."

Her "yes" to the dog was also a "yes" to herself. She purposed to fulfill her promise and become a woman of her word. Within moments, Laurie retreated over the worn road that had led her to the tumble-down homestead. But she wasn't alone on the return trip—a smelly, scraggly dog was now by her side.

2

The Facade

Laurie smiled as she recalled the first encounter with her dog that scorching summer day. We were still enjoying our walk, and the sparse flakes that had fluttered down around us earlier must have summoned their friends. The snow began falling in earnest. All sight and sound drew inward around us in a muffled veil of unspoiled silence. Laurie's eyelashes provided the perfect resting place for a few playful snowflakes.

"Look at this!" I held my palms skyward. Every flake that landed on my black knit gloves was a crystalline masterpiece. "Check out this one. Oh, look at this tiny baby on my finger!" The falling artistry offered a welcome respite, allowing Laurie to catch her breath.

Using her nickname, I asked my friend the obvious question. "So, tell me, Lou, you said earlier that your new dog was a wretched creature like you. What did you mean by that?"

Laurie took a deep breath and exhaled a groaning, wordless response that I recognized as the universal sound of "You don't want to know!"

"That good, huh?" My stifled laugh invited her to share more. "It's my dog," she said. "I could hide from everyone—but her." Laurie's blue eyes were pensive.

"Explain." With a single word, I pushed the door open for Laurie to release what was straining inside her heart.

In a voice I almost couldn't hear, more to herself, she said, "I didn't expect this—any of this."

—⁓—

On the long drive home, with her new dog settled on the seat next to her, Laurie looked through the windshield with a blank stare. She didn't feel elated or satisfied. She didn't even feel like a good person. Instead, she felt confused and numb, sad and empty.

The dog, although underweight and weak, had resisted getting into Laurie's car. Several times she tried to turn around and run back to the trailer. Frantic, she clawed through the sandy earth as she fought to leverage herself against being placed into an unknown vehicle. Lying on the seat, she panted in nervous gasps. Every time Laurie reached over to console her, the fearful dog squirmed away from her hand.

This dog doesn't even want to be touched.

Her large and wild eyes darted in every direction, as she tried to find a way of escape.

The stress of leaving the only home she's ever known must be triggering her anxiety. A new thought occurred to Laurie. *I wonder if she thinks she is going to die now.*

Laurie looked at the terrified dog, whose only response was trembling submission; the canine dared not look back. At that moment, something inside Laurie changed. Drop by drop, like melting ice, compassion for the frightened dog began to flow.

Wow, this dog has struggled for a long time. She has fought hard and survived so much. I don't really know how yet, but I can provide her with another chance. I know I can give this dog a new start, another try at this life. I can do that. I know I can do that.

As Laurie drove, juniper and sage rushed by in a swirl of monotone green. Their blended fragrance saturated the sultry heat. Laurie glanced over at the dog and sighed. She knew there was only one reason she had decided to rescue this homely, starving, foul-breathed creature.

I wish I could say I am keeping this broken girl because I in-

stantly fell in love with her. Perhaps, in time, that will come. I made the decision to bring her home because she needs my help. She's so thin and neglected. I couldn't leave her there. I couldn't look the other way and convince myself that she would be okay. I couldn't walk away…and do nothing.

She rubbed the back of her hand across her forehead and tried to untangle her thoughts from her emotions.

Laurie despised the fact that she chronically lived in a place that was dictated by her feelings. She resolved to move beyond her emotion, beyond the teetertotter of what she felt versus what was true. The truth was simple: this dog needed her help, she could give it, and she chose to. Emotional quicksand had enslaved Laurie for too long. Now she wanted to base her decision on what was needed, not on what she needed to feel.

Drop by drop, like melting ice, compassion for the frightened dog began to flow.

To confirm her decision, Laurie repeated her conclusion: *I'm helping this dog because it's simply the right thing to do.*

—⁓—

Ever since she was a little girl, Laurie had carried a heart full of vast and vivid dreams. She always had a clear picture of the person she wanted to be and what she wanted to do. She hoped her life would stand for something greater than herself. With the untarnished innocence of a child, she adopted her generation's aspirations to be happy, beautiful, and prosperous, to raise a family and change her world. Laurie loved children and teaching and hoped to combine those two elements in her future. What she wanted to do for humanity would matter. It would make a difference. She would make a difference.

With those ideals firmly established, Laurie never could've imagined that twenty years later she would be so far from the aspirations of her youth. Her heart had become the source of a turbulent, unceasing churn of doubt. She was beset with feelings of uncertainty and constant questioning of how her life could have strayed so far off track.

What she wanted to do for humanity would matter. It would make a difference. She would make a difference.

From an outsider's viewpoint, Laurie had it all. Raised in a loving home, she worked a respectable job, maintained an active social life, and attended church on Sundays. In contrast, her view from inside proclaimed the truth: she was profoundly lonely. Inside the bare walls of her life, beyond the scrutiny of all others, a young woman wandered alone, lost in a desert of isolation.

Nearly all her adult life had been consumed with the pursuit of fulfillment, worth, and love. In a give-and-take world, Laurie soon learned that if she wanted to feel valued and loved, it was going to cost her. Her desperation to fill these needs was matched only by her vain attempts to satisfy them. Slowly, her resistance to stand against self-destructive habits caved in under the weight of their promised consolations.

In an effort to quell her insatiable desire to be valued, accepted, and loved, Laurie gradually relinquished her moral code. She fought less and less to retain a place of virtue. Instead of pursuing her dreams, she yielded to the destructive flow of drifting downstream. By doing so, every new twist in her logic led her to make one detrimental decision after another. Each destructive choice ushered her deeper into the hollow wasteland of loneliness. Outwardly her childhood ideals had become her self-fulfilling prophecy. To others, she looked happy, she looked beautiful, she looked prosperous. The truth of who she was lay barren and buried deep inside her.

On the inside, Laurie was dying.

Thus she began a personal search for anything that would fulfill her, anything that would give her vacant existence meaning. First, Laurie bought into the lie that if she were thinner, then she would be closer to society's standard of beauty and worthy of everlasting love. Sadly, the result was not fulfillment but utter imprisonment. Laurie became a slave to her image, her weight, and a gnawing obsession with food. She dragged the shackles of a distorted self-image.

Needing to flee her confused and troubled heart, Laurie ran. She focused on escaping to a new place where she could make a fresh start. Her actions looked to those around her like a glorious, innovative chapter of adventure and travel. Surely, gaining an education abroad, exploring luxurious locations, and dining on exotic cuisine would boost the bottom line of her value as a progressive woman. With each move, she hoped to find the perfect place where she would finally fit in, where she might be freed from her plague of loneliness.

When it came to building friendships in these new regions, Laurie understood it was only a matter of time before she was discovered as a fraud. She didn't know how to be a friend or live selflessly for others. In each new place, she realized it would be only a few months before her previous mistakes and selfish breakdowns would overtake her once again. Her ability to sustain a lasting relationship was always undermined by the false exterior she huddled behind. She was certain that once people glimpsed beyond her thin veneer, they would be disgusted by what they saw. To spare others the loathing and her own self the shame, she made it a habit to move on before anyone really knew her. Laurie repeated this shallow, transient practice for several years to keep from facing her broken past.

With each move to a new location, Laurie allowed herself to be pulled into different and sometimes alternative crowds. She often mimicked those around her by forsaking who she was in exchange for what she believed others wanted her to become. For a brief phase, she imitated the glamorous crowd but was flatly rejected by their self-entitled ways.

It was nearly effortless for her to find a niche in the earthy spiritual-energy group, but their strange self-righteousness eventually drove her away. Laurie also stumbled into the angry, rebellious crowd, where no one was ever at fault. Here, her moral code slackened even further as she adopted the easy habit of simply blaming others for what she didn't want to change. By doing so, she never had to take responsibility for her own destructive choices. It wasn't long before partying and promiscuity became a normal part of Laurie's life. In a sad moral bargain, she believed that if she hung out in trendy places and could show her peers that she was hip, funny, and engaging, maybe then they would accept her as a friend.

The price of becoming a valuable woman climbed to ever-increasing heights with every new boyfriend she allowed into what was left of her parceled-out heart. Every relationship began with the same euphoric high, driven by a false hope that this time it would be different. But it wasn't different. Each relationship ended with the same crushing low, hallmarked by a greater sense of emptiness. Each failed liaison left Laurie with less of herself and more of the wasting disease of loneliness that devoured her very core. Her ever-changing life as a chameleon, trying to become the woman each man dreamed of, was costing Laurie her soul.

Although her facade remained glossy, intact, and beautiful, Laurie's skillfully hidden true self always felt churned up, troubled, and empty. Because the attractive approach didn't satisfy her, she even tried a short season of its polar opposite. Complete trashiness became her trademark. She dressed in tight, revealing clothing and wore heavy, dark makeup. She matched her internal pain with external piercings in a desperate effort to disguise her constant fear of rejection.

All of Laurie's efforts to fill her heart with love, value, and purpose brought only fleeting moments of relief. She was starving, and everything she tried to feed herself brought only a savory aroma, merely enough to make her stomach knot and her mouth flood with the anticipation of something real. But nothing she could produce was real. She was terrified to take an honest look into her own soul. She felt certain that if she did, nothing would stare back at her but the bottomless, empty gaze of an emotional refugee.

The sum of Laurie's endeavors to bear her brokenness left her with even greater wounds. Every self-promoting effort to restore her shattered heart resulted in greater devastation. All her frantic and manipulative cries for help fell upon the deafness of her peers. Everything she did to rescue herself failed. So she did the next best thing. She became a master of deception. There was no smile or angry expression she couldn't hide behind. Sadly, the soul she was most deceiving was her own.

Even though the world shouted, "This is as good as it gets, this is all there is," Laurie knew that she wanted something more. She struggled to hold on to the hope that perhaps there was something more. There must be something more.

Insidiously, her vices took over—until one day Laurie realized she was no longer in control of the ploys she used to gain what she needed; they were in control of her. In that black season, Laurie finally recognized that she was being pulled into the throat of a behemoth. The monster that sought to destroy her had a ravenous mouth that knew no satisfaction. Its jagged teeth closed around her, paralyzing her with despair. The sharp fangs that gripped her had names: guilt, hopelessness, shame, selfishness, pride, fear, sorrow, worthlessness.

There must be something more.

Although Laurie knew about God, she had chosen not to turn to him. She had mistaken God for a church, a group of people, and a set of rules. When they failed her, she believed that God also had failed her. God felt too far away to satisfy her needs. Even though she had been raised in a Christian home, she had never genuinely embraced her own relationship with God. Instead, she assumed only enough Christianity to make her look good when she needed to. Laurie learned how to wear faith like an accessory, choosing to bring it out only to complement her exterior appearance in order to blend in with others who had a deeper faith than her own.

On the outside, Laurie looked righteous and together, but inside she was in turmoil. She had never worked to cultivate genuine faith; she had never harvested genuine peace. She had come to the private conclusion that if God had plans to do something good in her life, he would have to prove himself to her. He would have to show her in a tangible way, according to her expectations, that he was real.

—⁂—

Driving up to a fork in the road, Laurie suddenly had to choose which direction would lead her back home. *What am I doing? Trying to make myself feel better by rescuing a dog? Even if it's the right thing to do, am I still doing it for the wrong reasons?* Laurie acknowledged her attempt to fill the void in her heart with an unselfish act of benevolence. So far she didn't feel any better. In fact, she felt worse.

She had pushed her blackness so far down into the caverns of her soul that she had come close to convincing herself that her heart was healing, that everything was going to be all right. When she looked at the ragged and rejected dog, instinctively she knew that this creature was a four-legged reflection of herself.

Laurie still felt unsettled about the decision she had just made. She didn't question whether she had done the right thing. Her only real question was whether she was the right one to do it. In an unconscious gesture of reassurance, Laurie reached across the seat and placed a gentle hand on the dog's back. The dog shifted her weight, trying to move away. Laurie kept her hand quietly in place until the dog lay still. Without a word, she ran her hand over the smooth top of her dog's head, attempting to ease away both of their fears.

Instinctively she knew that this creature was a four-legged reflection of herself.

"Sweet dog, you can relax now. You're going to be okay. Everything is going to be all right. I'm going to take care of you. I don't know how, but I'm willing to try. Rest easy. We're going to work this out together."

—⁓—

It was nearly dark when Laurie and I rounded the bottom of the ranch driveway. Old-fashioned lanterns hung in the twilight, beckoning us to follow them up the hill toward the promise of a warm fire. The snow had stopped falling, furnishing a sanctuary of silence. Reflecting on all she had said, Laurie snuggled her hands into her coat pockets and confided, "In that moment, my life was about to be permanently changed—by a dog."

3

The Choice

Another hot and dusty day was coming to a close on the ranch. After receiving hugs and words of encouragement, a giggling stream of kids trickled down the long driveway. The staff and I combed over the ranch, each seeking to rake, scoop, or sweep the areas we were responsible for.

I coiled the water hose on our grassy hill and picked up crushed paper cups. The afternoon breeze had hidden them in the rabbitbrush that flanks the green knoll. Only moments earlier, the now mangled cups had been the weapons used in a spontaneous, squealing water fight. The ambush had been waged between some of my staff and a group of mischievous and now soaking wet kids. It had been such a good day. In fact, any afternoon spent in the company of children is a good day.

I corralled a herd of mashed cups in my arms and made my way down the hill toward a garbage can by the barn door. When I released the cups over the can, a few renegades bounced off the rim and dropped to the ground.

Any afternoon spent in the company of children is a good day.

Laurie, having just swept the boardwalk, came toward me with broom in hand. "Aha!" She laughed and pinned the stray cups to the ground before the breeze could scatter them again.

"Thanks, Lou." I picked up the last rebels and tossed them in the trash.

She made use of her fake western drawl. "Glad I could help ya, ma'am."

We laughed and talked about some of the highlights of the day, and then I saw Laurie's expression turn thoughtful.

"Do you have a minute?" she asked.

Over the years, I've observed from my staff, friends, and family that this statement is far less a question than it is a plea to be heard. "Sure, let's head up to the top of the hill." I gestured sideways with my head.

We walked the short distance to the highest place we could find and, without grace, collapsed on the cool grass. I gazed across the lowlands toward the rising Cascade mountains, grateful for the chance to be still. Each of the peaks and glaciers, valleys and crevasses, took me on an instant, reminiscent journey of hiking, skiing, or mountaineering.

I stretched out on the grass and raised one arm toward Laurie. "Speak to me," I said with mock drama that matched my goofy smile.

True to her nature, Laurie laughed and then shook her head. "No, it's nothing big. I just wanted to tell you some really cool things that have been happening between my new dog and me."

"I'd love to hear what's been going on. Fire away!"

"By speaking out loud what I'm learning, it makes it more real, more permanent in my life. Know what I mean?" Her eyebrows accented her question.

I nodded in agreement.

"Well, once I brought my dog home, everything changed. She wasn't just scared. She was really sick and weak and needed my help to recover. I wasn't sure how things were going to work out, but within a few days I could tell she'd decided she could trust me. For some crazy reason, she chose to like me and wanted to play with me and sleep on my bed during her recuperation. Then, I believe, she started to love me…and I chose to love her back. She wasn't the cool blue-eyed dog I had hoped for, but I started to see all that she was—a homely, kind, and loving dog. In a short amount of time, we've become really good friends."

I couldn't contain the broad smile that I felt spreading across my face. "Well, look at that. Good for you, girl, for stepping up. It matters more than you know. Whether she chose to love you or not wouldn't have changed the fact that you did the right thing, and now something wonderful is happening because of it."

Once I brought my dog home, everything changed.

Laurie plucked several blades of grass. "I didn't think it was possible to become such good friends with a dog in such a short amount of time. I guess it took me a bit to realize that I needed to let go of my expectations and just accept her as she was."

I agreed. "Honestly, I doubt there's a creature on this earth that does exactly what you've just described better than a dog. No matter how badly we fail them, they just keep accepting us for who we are and love us anyway."

"Yeah, she's so much better at that than I am, but I'm learning. Wait! Make that, 'we're learning *together.*'"

"That's the spirit!" I laughed and tossed a few blades of grass her way.

"There were so many changes my 'Aussie girl' and I needed

to adjust to, like when I decided to rename her. Her old owner had called her Angel, which I didn't feel suited her at all. Besides, I wanted her to have a new name to identify her new start with me. I wanted her to know she was mine, that she belonged to someone. After lots of thought, I finally chose Chiquita Mia, which is Spanish for 'my little girl.' I knew that Mia was a very different sounding name from the one she had known before. Still, I felt confident that we could make the transition together."

I tested the name. "Mia. It's beautiful. I think it fits her well. Good job."

Laurie laughed a bit. "Even though Mia is nothing like what I had hoped for, she has stolen my heart. After spending time with her, all my selfish expectations seemed so small, so ridiculous. I'm ashamed I ever felt that way. Mia was homely, she was skinny, and she was stinky. But she was also kind, quiet, and gentle."

Love is not a feeling but a choice.

Laurie appeared to be talking more to herself than to me now. "She's becoming a true friend and a little dog that I'm growing to care for very much.

"And, get this—she has reminded me that love is not a feeling but a choice."

4

The Calling

I n an effort to accustom her dog to the sound of her new name, Laurie used it often—very often.

"Mia-Mia-Mia!" she'd call.

The instant her dog would turn toward her, Laurie would deluge her with praise.

"Good girl, Mia!" She reached to stroke the top of Mia's head. "Good dog, Mia."

By making the whole process a game, Laurie hoped to create a fun time of bonding. Laurie added entertaining spontaneity to the renaming process by singing "Mia songs."

Famous on the ranch for her ad-lib singing, Laurie is one of the true few who can make any person, place, or event into a song. Her original dog songs comprised whatever was playing on the radio, with Mia's name and acclaim skillfully woven in to the lyrics. At the time, because little else was known about Mia, most of Laurie's off-the-cuff lyrics featured the themes of her sweet dog's smile or bad breath.

Every song ended the same, with Laurie dissolving into hilarious laughter.

With the car windows down and Mia's tongue flapping in the breeze, Laurie and her dog made quite the singing sensation wherever they went. The amused expressions of the drivers around her only increased Laurie's joy. She would belt out a song and then turn to the dog sitting next to her as if she expected Mia to bark out the next verse. Then she would crack up at her own silliness. For Laurie, motoring down the road while singing a catchy tune to her new dog was such playful fun.

Mia took it all in stride. Sometimes, though, she would drop her head and gaze up at her new master with huge, forlorn eyes. Laurie concluded it was her dog's way of saying, "Hey! My breath might be bad, but your singing is terrible!"

Laurie and her dog made quite the singing sensation wherever they went.

Laurie decided to test the many days of name training by exploring one of the numerous lovely parks in Bend. Once there, Laurie leashed her dog and headed toward the Deschutes River. She paused to stare at the deep blue Oregon sky, a cobalt pool of peace. It invited her to inhale a chestful of pure, abundant hope.

In an explosion of gold, rabbitbrush bloomed across the High Desert. The endless carpet of plush yellow flowers offered a soft landing for a multitude of butterflies. Laurie drank in the sheer wonder of the season, grateful for the refreshment it poured into her thirsty soul as she walked Mia along the banks of the river. In that peaceful moment, she leaned down to free Mia from her leash and let her take pleasure in simply being a dog.

When Mia realized that her master was going to release her, she wagged her entire body with the promising thrill of investigating this new world. Her pinballing course led her to every tree, bush, and clump of grass. Each one called out in competition for her inspection. Laurie smiled as her Aussie girl wound her way through the layered grasses along the river's edge. With the slinky grace of a working-class cattle dog, Mia moved in perfect harmony within the placid environment.

Laurie watched her dog. Mia was still scraggly, skinny, and smelly—still very much the same—but Laurie was not. Her heart was changing. She was beginning to love this unlovely dog.

The sun lowered toward the horizon, and purple shadows

lengthened across the grassy park grounds. An unforgettable day was drawing to a close, and it was time for the two of them to head home.

Laurie turned and started walking in the direction of her car. "C'mon, Mia, let's go!"

To her surprise, Mia didn't even look up.

"Mia-Mia-Miaaaaa!" Laurie called again as her dog continued on her rambling investigation of all things. "Mia! Come here!"

Finally Mia stopped, and momentary hope replaced Laurie's frustration. She breathed a sigh of relief when Mia hesitated and turned around to look at her. Laurie locked eyes with her dog. In the voiceless moment that followed, it became clear that Mia was making a choice, weighing what her next action would be.

Shall I listen to you or not? Shall I come to you? Or shall I go my own way?

Even from a distance, Laurie could see the immense battle in her dog's contemplation. In the stillness, they held each other's gaze. Then came a subtle change in Mia's demeanor—subtle but unmistakable. Her head dropped slightly, and her eyes shifted to the side; she had reached her decision. Laurie watched in dismay as her willful dog chose to turn around and trot away.

The next thirty minutes of trying to catch her new dog

were not pretty for Laurie. Mia ran toward the river, and Laurie jogged after her. When Laurie would get within arm's reach, Mia would dart away. Again and again, Mia evaded Laurie's attempts to catch her. Finally, Mia's antics caught the attention of a picnicking family, and several left their meal to help Laurie capture her wayward dog.

Once Mia succumbed to being leashed, the two of them walked toward the car. Laurie fumed. *Why couldn't you just come to me? Don't you know that every good thing you have, I've given you? Don't you know that you were starving to death and I stood in the gap for you and kept you from dying under a rusty car?*

Laurie was so aggravated by the time she reached her vehicle that she couldn't hold back her tears. After all the time they had spent together, after all the love Laurie had invested in her,

Don't you know that every good thing you have, I've given you?

after all her effort to give Mia a new home and a new life, Laurie couldn't believe that Mia would choose to ignore her. They were in this together. Why would she run away?

Laurie ranted. "Mia, don't you realize that I saved you? Don't you know that I was the one who rescued you from the misery you were in? Don't you know that I love you? Why did you run away from me?"

Recovering from her escapade, Mia sat panting, oblivious to Laurie's questions.

Laurie slammed the car door, put the key in the ignition, and drove her disobedient dog home.

During the drive back to her house, Laurie glanced across the car to the passenger seat. Mia sat fully at ease, bearing no guilt or frustration. It was obvious she was satisfied to watch the world stream by outside the window. In that moment, Laurie envied her dog. Clearly Mia was content, and Laurie was not. Mia had already moved beyond the park fiasco and was just happy to be with her master.

Laurie pushed her irritation aside and delved into a deeper issue that was cutting into her thoughts. Internal questionings surfaced.

Can I honestly blame Mia for not coming to me? For not really knowing me? For not understanding how much I love her?

Laurie had to acknowledge that she and Mia still had much to learn about each other. Mia didn't come to Laurie because she didn't yet know or trust the sound of her voice, nor did she understand the depth of Laurie's love. The reason became clear: Mia had not yet spent enough time in Laurie's presence to really know her.

In the silence of the drive home, a new awareness started to materialize in Laurie's heart. It was as if fragments from a faraway voice echoed inside, and she strained to make out the words. Laurie pulled into her driveway and turned off the ignition. She sat in the quietness, interrupted only by Mia's even breathing. Once the fragmented words formed into a message, the truth jolted Laurie's soul.

I am exactly like Mia.

Just as her dog had run away from her, she had run away from God. Instead of running to God, she had spent her life running after everything but God. How could she follow a voice she had heard but never taken the time to actually know? How could she expect God to lead her life when she had repeatedly chosen not to follow him? Just like her dog's relationship with her, Laurie had not yet spent enough time in God's presence to truly know him either.

Laurie looked into this reflection of truth and clearly saw that she—and only she—was responsible for the distance she felt between herself and God. Her heart became as heavy as it had when her beloved dog ran away. All this time, she had been angry with God because he seemed so far away when she needed him most. She could no longer blame God for all the years of feeling abandoned now that she had just seen a mirror image of what she must look like to him. All along, Laurie was the one who had been running away from him.

—∞—

"Truth is truth, no matter who delivers it," I said, rolling up onto my elbow to look at Laurie. "God is such a fox. Isn't it incredible how he uses the world around us, simple things really, to continually reveal his great love, purpose, and plan for our lives? It's almost funny that God would use a dog to teach a girl how to listen."

Laurie gazed out over the ranch. "All this time, I've been such a horrible, selfish person. I've pretended to be kind and caring but, in reality, only when it served me. In the short season I've been with her, Mia, in all her mangy awfulness, has been far more of a loving creature than I ever have. I am the wretched, mangy, awful one!

"How could I have been so foolish? After watching my dog look right at me, acknowledge my presence, and then willfully choose to turn around and go her own way, I now see that, from God's perspective, I've been doing the exact same thing. When I saw my dog bound away, I saw an accurate image of myself. That's what I've been doing for years. No wonder my life has been so messed up."

Sitting with her arms balanced across her knees, Laurie lowered her head and wept. I held back my desire to rush in to console her, to fix the problem, and waited in silence. I too have stood on thresholds of honest reflection. It is painful but necessary for growth. It doesn't feel good, but it is good. To move away from our difficult lessons too quickly, to not take time to understand and feel their weight, is to be robbed of their rich purposes.

While Laurie grieved, I put my hand on her knee and made small, comforting circles with my thumb. The sun sank low in the sky until it finally balanced on the jagged horizon. Laurie drew in deep breaths and began to collect herself. An exhausted sound escaped her lips as she employed her T-shirt sleeve to dry her face.

Still processing her thoughts, Laurie continued. "For years, my mind has been consumed with resentment toward God for allowing painful events in my life. All this time, I've conveniently chosen to be caught in a loop of challenging God with questions. Each one focused solely on me and what I wanted."

"What questions?"

"Oh, all my questions sound nearly the same: *Where is God when I need him? If God really loves me, why doesn't he make my hardships stop? Why doesn't he take me out of the storms that beset my life? Isn't that what real love does? Why doesn't he surround me with peace? When my troubles appear, why does God disap-*

pear? Why? Why? Why? That has been my constant, nagging interrogation."

Laurie placed her hands over her ears like a hear-no-evil monkey. "I kept saying, 'God! I can't hear you, I can't hear you!'" With her hands still covering her ears, she stopped and stared at me. "The truth is, I couldn't hear him because I didn't want to."

I nodded, not wishing to interrupt her momentum.

"What's also true is that I've been living pretty much my whole life just like my wayward dog. Because of Mia, I can clearly see that all along it was my own self-centered obsessions that plugged my ears and blinded my eyes from understanding God's perspective."

Laurie took a deep breath and sighed. "Now I'm beginning to get it. God never promises a perfect life—he promises perfect peace. I never understood the power of that statement as a kid because my life was easy then. And once I realized I needed God's perfect peace, I chose instead the fool's pursuit of a perfect life."

I hoped she would keep thinking out loud, so I said nothing and smiled to encourage her.

She lowered her chin and spoke to the ground. "I've been so dumb, I've been so selfish! No human voice could break through my wall of pride. It took a dog to show me what I've been doing and what I must look like to God."

She plucked a single blade of grass and methodically tore it into little pieces. "I think it's time for me to stop questioning and to start listening."

After more silence and many shredded blades of grass, I said, "It sounds like you're making some progress. So what are you hearing?"

"Well, because of Mia, I'm gaining perspective. The picture of my life has come into sharp focus. I've been treating God like a bank and going to him only in great anger or deep sorrow. Then I would beg or demand him to give me what I wanted: peace, love, comfort, health, finances—my list was long! I'm sad to say that when my requests were not met within my time frame, I would storm away and blame him for everything that had gone wrong in my life.

"Now, because of my sweet yet disobedient dog, I understand that God has been calling out to me for years. He has been answering my prayers all along. He just didn't answer them in a way that I recognized."

Laurie paused. "Because the reality is, I never recognized him."

"Wow." I looked directly into Laurie's eyes. "I'm so glad God brought you and Mia together. Who would have thought that a mirror could have four paws? What a sweet change of attitude we can assume when we understand that God is with us, whether we are running away from him or to him."

Laurie looked steadily back. "My dog has taught me that if I don't like where my life has ended up, I can only blame myself. Because, just like my dog, I'm the only one who can choose which direction I run."

God is with us, whether we are running away from him or to him.

5

The Lesson of Love

The long, hot days of summer slowly relinquished their rule, vanquished by the glory of fall. One chilly autumn evening, Laurie joined me in front of a crackling fire for a bowl of beef stew. Our workday was finished, and we were looking forward to catching up before she went home to Mia.

Laurie cupped a brimming bowl in both hands and held it close to her body. "Mmm, this is nearly as good as eating it. My hands were getting so cold before we came up to the house."

Stew bowls in hand, we moved to our small family room and settled on two leather couches I had purchased at a secondhand store. Laurie let out a contented sigh. "This has been a remarkable time for Mia and me. Almost every day brings a different challenge. What I have enjoyed most about this time is the softening I see in Mia."

"Softening? How so?" I blew the steam off my spoonful of stew.

"Well, apparently she has moved beyond the season of viewing me as a stranger who calls her by a weird name to being someone she actually trusts. Mia is accepting me, faults and all."

"What do you mean, 'faults and all'?"

Laurie rolled her eyes and let out her "Uh-huh" laugh, letting me know she was aware of my desire to get to the core of what she needed to talk about. "Well, this once skinny, unattractive dog no one else wanted has been changing my life one day at a time. She's managed to do what no friend, church, therapist, boyfriend, or self-help group has been able to do—ever." Her gaze drifted; she was lost in thought.

If only I could love me like my dog loves me.

I took another bite of my stew and raised my eyebrows in a comical fashion.

Laurie glanced up and caught my silly expression. She laughed and then said, "If only I could love me like my dog loves me. She ignores my false veneer and jumps right into the real me. I can tell Mia has grown to really love me. She is my scruffy, damaged dog, who is choosing to love this scruffy, damaged girl."

I smiled. "Lou, we all have our scruffy, damaged places. It's the process of healing, of growing beyond our shortcomings, that shapes who we can become. We each get to choose whether our hardships will ruin us—or refine us.

"Other than Christ, nobody's born perfect. Nobody gets everything right the first time. If we so choose, it is our scruffy, damaged-ness that can teach us so much. I'm able to think of little else that can drive us more quickly to a place of perseverance, forgiveness, and compassion. Honestly, as unpleasant as our weak and rough places are, they all can be used to teach us the antithesis of the very issues we struggle with."

Laurie's intent expression encouraged me to go on.

"For instance, growing through a time of unbearable stress can help you understand the true value of peace. By choosing to work through resentment and an unwillingness to forgive, we can learn a greater depth of forgiveness and love. Does that make sense?"

Laurie nodded in agreement.

"Girl, every hardship we face is an opportunity to either break down or break through. We choose the outcome. For each difficulty we struggle with, we decide if it will make us weaker or stronger."

Laurie spoke in earnest. "Because the relationship between Mia and me is safe and forgiving, I'm learning how to genuinely love. Unlike the love I had previously known in all my failed relationships, I'm discovering that real love has roots."

Her eyes brightened, and she set aside her stew bowl. "Day after day, my dog is showing me that nothing can grow without roots, including love." With one hand covering her heart and the other in a palm-up position, she began to recall the insights she was learning from her dog. "She shows me how honest love is like a tree; it stands firm and it perseveres through storms."

"How did you learn that from Mia?" I asked.

"Well, in the beginning, Mia ran away because she didn't really know me. But, as we built a relationship founded on trust, everything changed. No matter how late I get home, Mia's always thrilled to see me and greets me with joy. She's not unhappy when I'm exhausted and irritable; she still wants to lick my face. No matter how frustrated I might be with her, she looks beyond my shortcomings and accepts me right where I am."

In mouth-full-of-stew agreement, I pointed at Laurie with my spoon and nodded. She grinned and waited for me to swallow. "You're so right about real love having roots," I said. "Anything that lasts can't do so without having a solid base. Real love doesn't focus on another's faults; it reaches past that topsoil and sends down roots into what's real. When we do this with each other, we imitate the same strong support redwood trees give each other. Being from California, you've surely seen the redwood groves there."

Every hardship we face is an opportunity to either break down or break through.

"I have. They're incredible."

"Then you've noticed how they never grow alone. As tall as they are, if they stood alone, even minor winds would blow them over. Instead, they always grow in groves so they can intertwine their roots and anchor each other. By doing so, they literally hold each other up during violent storms. Genuine love does that; its roots reach beyond superficiality and entwine the very heart, soul, and essence of who we are one to another. In a very simple way, your dog has done this."

Understanding lit up Laurie's face. "Yes! Because of that, I no longer view my recovering dog as a homely creature that deserves my pity because she was rejected. Instead, I see her through a heart that is being changed by authentic love. I think it's because of her honest love for me that I no longer notice her imperfections. In my eyes she has become beautiful."

Laurie's words came quickly, energized by her rising enthusiasm.

"Although her outside has changed very little, my inside is being completely renewed. Mia isn't lovely because she has been miraculously transformed into this world's standard of beauty. She's beautiful to me simply because of who she is. She is showing me how to open my heart and love others in the same way."

Laurie nodded in apparent agreement with her own thoughts, and then her eyes focused on my face.

I lowered my bowl, letting her know she had my full attention.

True to her tender-hearted nature, Laurie's eyes began to glisten. A weak laugh escaped her lips. "Funny how all the previous relationships in my life have not been able to teach me what real love is—until I met and really got to know this dog. Love is not something I made happen between Mia and me. It's been like seeping water, drop by drop, moment by moment. I just fell in love with her. All her imperfections didn't stop me from loving her. In fact, they are some of the things I have grown to love most about her."

Laurie looked away, as if she were picturing Mia, and her expression softened. "I'm embarrassed to admit that I used to think she was ugly. The real ugly wasn't her—it was me, my attitude." Laurie sighed. "I look at her now and wonder, 'Who *couldn't* love this dog?' She's so cute, so sweet, so Mia."

She laughed. "Although I must confess, I could do without the terrible breath!"

Still cupping my hot bowl, I interjected, "Your life, from the outside, seemed so good, so full of love. It's amazing to me that it took a dog to show you how empty you really were."

Laurie wrinkled her nose. "I really thought I knew what love was. What a joke! My version of love was so conditional, so inconsistent." She paused. "You're right. It was through this little dog that I began to understand how love connects our hearts. How even through sickness, frustration, expense, and stinky breath, I still love my dog.

"Humans have so many shallow ideas of love. If things aren't pretty and perfect, we start looking elsewhere. Dogs don't do that. They possess a level of loyalty that most people will never fully understand. I sure didn't. It took a dog to teach me that authentic love, a love that connects hearts—even imperfect hearts—does exist."

Laurie's eyes sparkled.

"What else?" I asked, wanting to throw more fuel on her already blazing fire.

She picked up her bowl and, without taking a bite, plunged ahead. "Most of us have experienced love that walks away for something better when the imperfections become unbearable. But love that binds hearts and stands firm, no matter what comes, is genuine. The best part is that anyone can find it! Mia showed me this truth because she was unlovable by many people's standards, including my own shallow ideals, when I first met her. But now that I know her, I love her, authentically and unchangeably."

Laurie leaned forward. "Unlike many of my two-legged acquaintances, Mia didn't demand that I change to fit into her mold of what a real friend should be. She demonstrates that she loves me just as I am, faults and all. No matter how badly I fail her, her love never fails me. She always gives me her very best. There's nothing I can do to stop her from wanting to be with me. She's showing me the way of sincere love. I think my new challenge is to follow her example."

I picked up my Mason jar of water and tipped it in Laurie's direction in a redneck toast. "To lessons of love!"

Laurie smiled and lifted her jar to join mine. "Hear, hear!" She laughed and celebrated the moment with me by chugging a mouthful of water, then lowered her jar. "Plain and simple, my little

Love is a bridge that stands firm through difficulties and connects one heart directly to another, not because of how it looks, but because of what it is.

dog has consistently demonstrated how love is a bridge that stands firm through difficulties and connects one heart directly to another, not because of how it looks, but because of what it is."

6

The Diagnosis

Mia was not only thin, she was also sick. Besides the obvious issues of her weight, coat, and teeth, other health problems plagued her. After checking with various veterinary sources, Laurie took Mia to the Redmond Veterinary Clinic to clarify the cause of her dog's mysterious symptoms. Laurie followed the new veterinarian's recommendation and scheduled Mia to spend an entire day at the hospital for the most comprehensive exam they could give her.

A month later, Laurie and I had a chance to catch up on each other's lives while driving together in my black truck to a local feed store. It was then that she told me about the follow-up appointment at the veterinary clinic to find out what was troubling her dog.

"In the waiting room, I felt like a little kid in a Norman Rockwell painting, seated on a bench with my dog at my feet. I then sat in a cheerful exam room while Mia sprawled out on the shiny floor next to me. The entire clinic smelled like strong antiseptic, and the walls were covered with informational charts and encouraging sayings. On the counter in the exam room were lots of glass jars filled with all kinds of medical supplies. One jar especially caught my eye; it was filled with dog treats. I wondered if they had a jar filled with people treats too."

Laughing, I said, "I'm going to talk to them about that. I think they need a bucket full of M&M'S!"

"You're right! Or at least a jug of Starbucks!"

We gave each other a rancher high-five across the cab of my truck.

Antics aside, Laurie said, "When Dr. Shawn breezed into the room, his bright, upbeat demeanor couldn't conceal the fact that he was about to give me some very bad news."

My heart sank. Dr. Shawn was one of the primary vets for our ranch and also a dear friend, and I knew that expression all too well. In more than a dozen years of working with our rescued horses, some critically ill, Dr. Shawn has had plenty of opportunities to use the same expression with me. I've come to recognize it as his "This isn't going to be easy news to receive, so I will deliver it with as much optimism as I can" expression.

Nevertheless, I love Dr. Shawn and learned long ago to rely on his counsel.

Laurie took a deep breath, and I knew she was steeling herself to describe what followed.

—␣—

Dr. Shawn began with a smile. "Mia has not been spayed."

Laurie smiled back, puzzled by his comment. The previous owner had told her that Mia had been spayed.

"You'll need to make an appointment to have her spayed as soon as you can fit it into your schedule."

Laurie nodded. "Okay."

"And Mia has some extensive dental decay that will require several extractions followed by a good teeth cleaning."

Laurie had expected that news, but she was surprised that Mia's tooth damage was so pervasive. Mia was also going to require an expensive brand of dog food. Laurie listened as the list grew.

"In addition, Mia is going to need insulin injections twice a day."

"What do you mean? Insulin? Why would she need insulin?"

"Mia is suffering from an aggressive form of canine diabetes."

Each piece of news landed like a boulder on Laurie's heart.

"Laurie, her diabetes is severe. Mia's developing cataracts, and she's in the process of going blind."

"Blind? What? My dog is going blind?" Laurie's heart hadn't recovered from that boulder when the next giants began to fall.

Each piece of news landed like a boulder on Laurie's heart.

"Yes, Mia is going blind. As pressure continues to build in her eyes, there's a strong possibility she will also need, at some point, to have her eyes removed."

Laurie's jaw dropped as she looked up into the vet's face.

"There's more," Dr. Shawn said.

No, no, no more! Please, God, no more. The voice in her heart begged like a pleading child.

Dr. Shawn's voice was gentle. "Mia's blood work and glucose curves are…well, compelling."

Laurie's throat tightened. *No! Please, no… Don't use that tone.*

The vet's voice softened noticeably. "It might not be for a while, perhaps months or even years, but her test results are conclusive. Mia…is dying."

Laurie sat paralyzed, helpless against an unstoppable rush

of tears. *Why, God? Why? Why would you allow me to fall in love with her only to take her away?*

Laurie's face dropped into her hands in an effort to stop the sobs that began churning out of her chest. Crushed by an avalanche of sudden grief, Laurie felt like she couldn't move, couldn't breathe, couldn't think. All she could do was give in to the overwhelming weight of sorrow.

None of the jars on the counter held a cure for her breaking heart.

Dr. Shawn assured Laurie that just as with people, diabetes is serious but treatable. Mia could still have several years with a good quality of life.

"Just because Mia has a grave illness doesn't necessarily mean she should be put down immediately. Unless, of course, she develops signs of suffering. Or if you don't wish to pay for her continued care or be committed to administering insulin to her on a regimented basis."

Laurie took a deep breath. Through her tears the answer came without hesitation. "I have to try."

Her mind reeled in a myriad of directions. "If Mia is going blind, she'll run into things. Wouldn't that be considered pain and suffering?"

Dr. Shawn reassured Laurie with a gentle smile. "Blind people bump into things all the time. That's how they learn to adjust to their environment." His smile broadened. "I may be going out on a limb here, but I'm pretty sure they're okay with not being euthanized even though they bump their forehead or split their lip from time to time."

Laurie relaxed. The message was loud and clear. Together, she and Dr. Shawn would seek the very best care for Mia; each would keep a watchful eye on her and monitor her progress. As long as Mia maintained a healthy and happy life, all would be well.

Dr. Shawn and Laurie agreed on a mutual strategy that would provide the best life possible for her dog. Laurie could foresee a time when what would be best for her might not be best for her dog. She didn't want that responsibility to reside solely on her emotional fortitude, so she asked Dr. Shawn to guide her in making an informed decision when that time came.

They concurred that once Mia showed signs of untreatable pain, that would be the time to humanely end her life.

Please, God, show me how to do this. Show me how to take care of my precious girl.

As much as Laurie might wish for her precious companion to be with her always, she would not choose for her dog to suffer needlessly to satisfy her own selfish heart.

Laurie left the office armed with as much information as Dr. Shawn could give her. One thing was clear: Mia's diabetes would kill her eventually.

Please, God, show me how to do this. Show me how to take care of my precious girl so that our days together might be long.

—∿—

Even though Dr. Shawn had warned Laurie that the process of stabilizing insulin levels could sometimes be tumultuous, the month that followed was frightening. Finding the precise level of medication proved challenging for both woman and dog. Finally, after many glucose curves and daily observations, Laurie found a system that seemed to keep Mia balanced and healthy.

Laurie devoured information about canine diabetes and trained herself to know when Mia had too much insulin or not quite enough. She learned how to monitor her dog's levels of exercise and even how to handle a crash when Mia's insulin levels were too low.

Through it all, Mia remained steadfast in optimism. She never acted frustrated or grumpy about her ongoing treatments. She appeared to take all her new hardships in stride. Every moment in her life was a gift, and she seemed to know it.

Finally, after spaying, dental work, and the removal of her

hemorrhaging left eye, Mia began to thrive under her loving master's care. The once ragged and forsaken little dog Laurie had brought home only months before had transformed into a beautiful, glossy-coated friend of her soul.

Laurie remained true to the feeding schedule Dr. Shawn had laid out for her, and Mia mimicked The Little Engine That Could and gained an impressive twenty pounds. Oftentimes Laurie looked at her courageous dog in complete wonder and tried to comprehend how so much energy could fit into such a small and broken body. Mia proved daily just how resilient a happy heart could be.

—⁓—

Laurie smiled at me across the cab of my truck. "I think this whole episode with Dr. Shawn and all that Mia has endured is teaching me that what I once thought was impossible isn't. For so long, my first response to hard things was to simply run away from them. Because of Mia, I can see that by persevering, by really holding on, so much more is possible."

I nodded. "Someone recently told me that you should work like your dreams depend on you…and pray like they depend on God."

Laurie beamed. "Yes! I'm beginning to understand what that actually means."

7

The Three Things

Time dealt its ruthless hand just as Dr. Shawn had predicted with his bleak diagnosis: Mia was going blind. After the removal of her left eye, a massive cataract formed in her right eye, almost blocking what little vision she had left. It was difficult for Laurie to watch her girl slip into a world of darkness, but she found encouragement, hope, and bravery in an unlikely source—Mia herself.

Quite simply, Mia never gave up. She possessed an uncanny ability to keep bounding forward. Waking up to a new day was reason enough to drum her tail against the floor. When Mia sensed that Laurie was awake, she greeted her with good morning kisses all over her hands, asking to come up on the bed for her daily cuddles. True to her canine nature, Mia still begged for treats as often as she believed she could gain one. Life was good.

The games they played together changed, but not the fun. Laurie took advantage of open grassy areas to play a blind dog's version of hide-and-seek, with Laurie dancing around her dog and whistling. Mia would respond by leaping after her in large, crazy patterns. Another favorite was when Laurie would slap the ground around her dog's feet. Mia would bite at the ground and try to catch her master's hands with her paws. The grand finale would come when Mia turned onto her back and Laurie would gently wrestle with her. Mia would grab Laurie's wrists in her toothy grin and roll around in pure elation.

Mia could always be counted on for one of the biggest dog smiles of the day when Laurie would release her from the leash during their walks. Gripped by the anticipation of being free, Mia would circle tightly while wildly wagging her tail. With her head lifted and mouth open, she would make sure that her master saw the size of her big smile.

Mia's intense love of freedom posed an obvious and paradoxical problem for both owner and pet. Her birthright and design dictated that she be a high-energy dog. From Mia's perspective, submitting to a tether constituted her idea of prison and just didn't make sense.

Yet Laurie's perspective as her caretaker and protector was

vastly different. Because of Laurie's love for her dog, it was her job to keep Mia safe, to shelter her from harm. Laurie was to be her guard, her eyes. In a world that was best for Laurie, Mia would remain on a leash for the duration of her days. That would keep Mia safe and stop Laurie from worrying about her.

Mia's intense love of freedom posed an obvious and paradoxical problem for both owner and pet.

But was that always what was best for Mia?

———— ⁓ ————

"Knock-knock," Laurie called from the front door of my home.

I motioned for her to come into my office and take a seat while I wrapped up a phone call. She flopped into a rusted yellow chair, one of my two antique metal chairs befitting a ranch office. Laurie leaned into the red fleece blanket thrown over the chair and pulled out her notes for our informal meeting. I watched her eyes roam the walls around us. Each was filled to capacity with an assortment of artwork from loved ones, cavalry bits, old studded leather tack, and other western antiques and memorabilia.

Laurie appeared captivated by my mountain pictures.

Majestic photographs of Mount Rainier and Mount Shasta were bordered by shots I took while climbing them. The two ice axes I had used hung between the pictures. Several images showed crevasses so massive that my house could easily fit inside their icy expanse.

Laurie kept scanning, and then she broke out with a snicker. She motioned toward a humorous plaque and mouthed, "Hey, I need one of those."

I hung up the phone and spun around in my chair to see which item had amused her. It was a faux Wild West sign inscribed with an old western script. I read it aloud: "Put your big girl panties on and deal with it!"

We laughed, nodding in agreement.

I pointed with my thumb and said, "I love this sign because it reminds me to not take the little rough spots throughout the day so seriously. As women, we can get so hung up on such small, ridiculous things. As silly as this sign is, it really does encourage me to make big girl choices over the decisions I face while sitting at my desk."

"Ah, speaking of choices," Laurie said, "boy, has my little dog been showing me the true impact of the choices we make in this life. Because of her sudden blindness, I've had to keep her on a leash, and she can't stand it! It's been tough on us both.

She wants her freedom; I want her safety. She wants to be the active dog she once was, and I want her to learn how to travel through this world without being destroyed by it."

Laurie glanced out the window, where a dozen sparrows and juncos feasted at a feeder. She laughed a bit, more to herself than to me. "It's kinda weird. So much of the dilemma I'm having with my dog is the same as what my parents once had with me."

"What do you mean by that?"

"Well, you know the old adage, 'No parent can raise their child in a padded room'? Man, that has been ping-ponging around in my head these days."

"How so?"

"I've been trying to figure out the best way to teach Mia to find her way through this season of her life. Now that she is almost totally blind, how do I guide her without doing everything for her? How do I allow her to learn from her own mistakes without being harmed by them? Now I understand how hard this must have been for my parents when I had more selfish desires than sense. I wanted to push against their guidance and test the limits of my freedom."

I laughed. "Why, I've never done that! I was the perfect child! Completely obedient in every way. Just ask my sisters. They'll confirm that's absolutely true—right after they pick themselves up off the floor from laughing nearly to death!"

After our hilarity subsided, Laurie's gaze dropped to the nubby oatmeal carpet. I could see she was drifting in thought again. I couldn't help but wonder if she was contemplating a specific moment of conflict with her parents.

Rallying her reflections, she looked up at me. "I keep questioning whether or not to let Mia off her leash. By constantly restraining her, I wonder, *Is it safe for her body?* Maybe, but it does restrict nearly all her natural exercise. Is it safe for her mind? Nope! She tells me that every time I clip her leash to her collar. Once Mia's on line, she acts like I've just slammed a prison door in her face. She hates it!

"I don't know what to do. I do know that for my dog to exist in this world of blindness, she has to be able to learn, adapt, and grow within it. I think that can only happen if she's allowed to explore the environment she's going to live in. Maybe then she can discover how to deal with it, one step at a time, right?" I could tell Laurie was asking for my permission as much as my opinion.

I took the bait. "Hmm, I think you're right. Just like you love to play the piano, this would be the same as knowing how to play in your head, but never practicing. You'll never really learn how to play unless you practice what you know."

"That's what I think! I couldn't live my life restricted by a three-foot line either. I've come to the conclusion that trying to shelter her by keeping her on a leash the rest of her life is doing her no favors; that's living in an unrealistic bubble world. I need to train her to live in the real world—the world she can't see with her eyes. This world has challenges and dangers. Her life is full of sharp edges, drop-offs, and a wood-burning stove. She needs to learn to listen to my voice of guidance and then steer around those potential dangers on her own. I feel like the best course of action is to train her to be obedient while she is on the leash and even more so when she is off."

I need to train her to live in the real world—the world she can't see with her eyes.

—————

With the deterioration of Mia's remaining eye, Laurie's presence and purpose in her life took on a fresh focus. She determined to help Mia develop the ability to survive in a new and different way.

Mia had already proved that she could overcome with ease the obstacles within her home and backyard without a leash. Since Mia would be off line in unknown environments while in her master's presence, Laurie needed to teach Mia to know and do three things: trust, believe, and listen. Mia must trust

Laurie's eyes to become hers. She must believe in Laurie's decisions. And she must listen to Laurie's voice. The only way Mia would able to accomplish these things is if she was allowed to practice them.

After many rehearsals, Laurie took Mia to the impressive Oregon Coast, with its miles of empty seashore. It was the perfect place to teach Mia how to trust, believe, and listen. Laurie could think of no setting more inspiring for coaching her friend.

Once the two of them arrived at the beach, Laurie released her wriggling dog from her leash. Mia was thrilled! She bounced around Laurie in big goofy leaps, always blindly looking up in the direction of where she believed her master's face might be. Mia's ecstatic body language seemed to shout, "Thank you!" Then, true to her species, she set off to investigate her new surroundings.

Fully living up to its reputation, the magnificent Oregon Coast delivers, no matter what the weather. The gray skies that day only added to the deepening sense of drama created by the heavy surf. Towering spires of black basalt rose like timeless cathedrals within the exploding waves. The cold wind whipped Laurie's hair and tore at her clothing. She braced herself against the torrent and mused, *Days like these make me know I'm alive!*

Laurie hurried to join Mia. While strolling along the beach, she watched her dog approach potentially dangerous chunks of driftwood.

"Careful!"

Mia hesitated and turned slightly toward the sound of her master's voice.

Laurie continued to warn. "Careful, careful!"

In a surprisingly short time, Mia learned that *careful* meant "move forward slowly."

Laurie was pleased with Mia's responses to her cues.

"Good girl, Mia!" Laurie called out praises for each good choice her clever dog made. Excited and proud of Mia's progress, Laurie added other commands such as "wait" and "stay." When Mia needed to step over something to avoid a hazard, Laurie added "step" to her list of commands.

Satisfaction filled Laurie to see her blind dog having so much fun. With minimal coaching from her master, Mia was a happy dog again, and she raced from one point of interest to another. Anyone watching her run along the beach would not have known Mia was blind. Laurie smiled as she watched her dog discover one captivating scent after another. *This day might not be long enough for Mia to explore it all.*

Laurie walked on the furrowed sand and took notice of every rock and shell displayed on the grainy expanse. The sun's gentle warmth had broken through the gray and combined with the wind-driven salt on her cheeks. With hands nestled in her jacket pockets, Laurie reveled in deep, wordless joy at being in this timeless place with her dog.

During their walk, dog and woman approached a cove harboring logs that had washed up among the large basalt rocks. The ebbing surf had carried the sand out from under the stones and wood, leaving beautiful curves and valleys around each of the obstructions. Although an intriguing place for Laurie, it was a dangerous place for Mia. Laurie drew in a deep breath, strengthening her resolve to guide her dog. With one cautionary command after another, she steered her blind dog through the rocky maze.

Laurie continued to call out directional advice but noticed a subtle change in her dog. Mia was not responding as quickly as she had been earlier. She was turning her head back less and less to listen to her master's voice. In fact, Mia's body would stiffen a little with every word of caution. Her actions told Laurie that she was resisting the barrage of instructions. Eventually, she stopped and looked in Laurie's direction. It was as if she were shouting back, "Oh, for goodness' sake! What danger? It's the beach!"

Laurie raised her voice. "Mia, wait!"

Mia turned and began to walk down the beach, a clear canine response that yelled "C'mon! Will ya quit holding me back and just let me have some fun?" She trotted the other way, utterly disregarding her master's voice.

Laurie sighed.

Only moments later, Mia took one too many steps in the wrong direction and tumbled right over the sandy ledge Laurie had been trying to help her avoid.

"Mia!" Laurie scrambled over to the four-foot embankment where her treasured friend had just tumbled. Laurie saw that Mia had bitten her tongue.

Before Laurie reached her, Mia regained her footing and was moving away again.

"Mia, it doesn't have to be this hard! Please stop! Girl, you can avoid all of this pain. Mia, please listen to me! You can't see—I can! Baby, trust my eyes and my voice." Laurie jogged after her dog, determined in her commitment to offer guidance. Mia moved away like a stubborn child and began to run from her master.

"Mia! Listen to me! Careful, careful!"

Laurie winced as Mia ran headfirst into a large washed-up stump.

Watching her dog crash made Laurie's stomach hurt.

Laurie was undeterred and continued to call after her dog. Mia recovered fast from her impact with the stump, only to turn and run into a huge rock. Even from a distance, Laurie saw that her dog's nose was bleeding.

Laurie pleaded, "Oh, Mia, please listen…please!" If voice commands were going to work, her canine friend must choose to trust her.

Without warning, scenes from Laurie's past failures moved through her head. She conceded that it was not words that changed her actions—it was consequences.

Sometimes it's the bloody noses in life that teach us the most.

After several more painful encounters with immovable beach debris, Mia seemed to have had enough of her own way. Quite suddenly, Laurie's voice resumed its authority. Mia's actions proved she'd had a change of heart. Once again, she began to listen to her master's warnings of impending danger. Mia decided that she had more fun, more security, and fewer bloody noses when she didn't just hear her master's voice but actually listened, responded, and obeyed.

Sometimes it's the bloody noses in life that teach us the most.

Laurie marveled at the changes in her dog.

In just a few short minutes, Mia had learned something

remarkable—something that had taken Laurie a lifetime to try to understand. Mia had chosen to allow her master to be her eyes, to believe in her master's decisions, and to listen to her master's voice. Outside of a few minor bumps and bruises, Mia made it look easy to trust in a voice emanating from someone she could not see.

—⁓—

I leaned back in my office chair and clapped. "Yeah, Mia! Well done, little dog! Well done!"

With a small laugh, Laurie agreed and placed her notes on the old Hoosier cabinet beside her. Quite suddenly, a slight frown pinched her face; I sensed she was sifting through all that she had observed of Mia's behavior. "When it comes to trust, believe, and listen, how can that kind of faith be so easy for my dog…but so hard for me?"

She opened her hands and lifted them toward the ceiling. "My dog isn't teaching me to sit and stay, but to move forward in action—to trust, believe, and listen. Before my eyes, Mia has demonstrated that it doesn't matter if I can see what lies ahead of me. It only matters that I trust, believe, and listen to the God who does."

8

The Light

The ring of my cell phone tugged my heart away from the Oregon Coast, with Laurie and Mia, and back to my office, where her story had first started. The number on the tiny screen read "Troy," my sweet boyfriend, my champion, the man I had married almost thirty years ago. Always eager to speak with him, I excused myself and took the call. Laurie signaled that she was going into the kitchen to get a glass of water. I smiled at her and raised my fingers in a "make that two glasses, please" gesture.

My conversation with Troy had concluded by the time Laurie returned with two Mason jars filled to the brim. Without a word she handed me a jar, and we both took long drinks. I sensed that she had more to share about all that had happened at the coast.

I spoke first. "To trust, listen, and believe takes time and practice. For most of us, it doesn't just happen. I think it's simply amazing that a dog can learn that in such a short amount of time. Kinda makes you want to start following your dog instead of her following you, doesn't it?"

Laurie smiled but did not look up. Her expression was one that I have come to recognize as her organizing-my-thoughts look. After a moment, she said, "Just like Mia ignored me that day on the beach, I have ignored God.

"That evening, I met up with some friends at their campsite. After dinner we decided to go for a walk on the beach. Mia was tired,

To trust, listen, and believe takes time and practice.

so I tucked her in to the dog bed in my car." Laurie paused. "The Oregon Coast is such a powerful place for so many reasons. One of the things I love most about it is how incredibly dark it is at night. It's one of my favorite places to go star-spinning."

"Star-spinning? What's that?"

"You know, looking up into the deep night sky, putting your

arms straight out, and spinning around and around until you can't stand up anymore. I used to do it when I was a little girl in California. My favorite part was falling backward into the sand and watching the stars circle in crazy patterns across the sky."

I laughed in acknowledgment. "I used to do that during my skiing days as a kid, except I did it while looking up at falling snow."

Laurie flashed me a knowing grin. "Only a few times in my life have I seen a sky as full of stars as this particular night. It was unbelievable. There were so many stars that they reached all the way down to the horizon. I felt surrounded by them. We spun around and around with our faces turned up toward the sky. Then we lay down in the sand and watched the most awesome show of dancing stars. After they stopped spinning, I got up and ran and danced and celebrated the beautiful night and the wonderful feeling of being with friends who loved God and loved me."

Laurie paused and looked away, apparently reliving the moment and the beauty of it all. "When it was finally time to leave the beach, we had to walk about a quarter of a mile under a deep canopy of trees. It was incredibly dark. I couldn't see a thing! Thankfully, Karen had thought to bring a flashlight. She walked in front and led us up the trail. My friend Risa followed her closely, and I stumbled along in the very back."

"Yikes, girl, I've been on the beach at night and it *is* dark!"

"I could see where Karen was walking. She had the light, so I kept looking ahead over her shoulder to see every root, rock, and hole. But by the time I reached the same hazards, the ground under my feet was completely black. Karen's light helped me stay on the path, but I was constantly tripping and stumbling, always fighting for my balance. I had no light of my own to help me. The farther we walked up the path, the more dangerous it became. Every time I lost my footing, I just got more and more frustrated."

"And when it's that black, even your equilibrium gets a little sideways."

"It was so hard! And right when I wanted to scream out loud, a thought flashed through my mind. *My life is just like this.* I had been stumbling in the darkness, and I desperately needed my own light, my own relationship with God.

I desperately needed my own light, my own relationship with God.

"Right there, on the dark trail, I prayed a simple prayer. I acknowledged to God that all this time I had been living my life in the darkness. I told God that I didn't want to live like this anymore. So I asked if he would show himself to me, if he would give me his light. And then…he did.

"At times, there have been people around me who knew God and shone with his light. By using the light of another instead of my own, I had no idea what lay ahead. Even though others offered gentle leadership and gave me ideas of what I was supposed to do, I would still get discouraged and often just go my own way. Apart from God, there is only darkness. Looking back, I can now see that those were the darkest and loneliest times of my life."

I nodded. "It always amazes me that we know we can't successfully travel this life on our own but that knowledge alone isn't enough to stop us from trying anyway. We still keep choosing to thrash around in the dark."

Laurie's gaze shifted toward the window, and I saw a shadow of a smile. "That night was a turning point in my life. It was the moment I became fully aware of how much I desire God to lead me, to show me his light. I want to know who God is. He heard my simple prayer, and for the first time, I could see his light and not my darkness."

I leaned back in my chair and opened my hands. "Wow, Lou! What a powerful picture! You could've continued to respond with the same old frustration, the same old evasion, the same old excuses—but you didn't. Way to go. I'm so deeply proud of you."

Laurie glanced back outside at some finches at the bird

feeder. "It's time, you know? Time to stop pretending. How ridiculous—and yet how wonderful—that everything I've ever learned in the past about God was clarified in that moment of walking in the dark. Just like Mia chose to trust me, it was time for me to choose to trust God. I needed to demonstrate confidence, not only in my heart but also with my actions, that God would lead me with his light. It was time for me to believe that no matter how far I had fallen away from God, there was no darkness so deep that I could fall beyond his willingness to be my light."

With my hands folded under my chin, I gazed across my office at Laurie. I wondered if she knew just how much she had moved me. What a joy it was for me to share in her tears and laughter. At that moment, I knew that

Just like Mia chose to trust me, it was time for me to choose to trust God.

no parent on earth could be more proud than I was of my friend's growth and triumphs.

Laurie's glance drew back from the window and focused on me again. "If I'm going to trust, believe, and listen to God, and if I'm going to walk in his light, I must first do one thing: I must choose to. Like my precious Mia discovered, it hasn't helped me at all to simply know what I should be doing. I need to *do* it. I kinda feel like a less-than-bright kid who's been presented a gift my entire life, but I kept choosing not to receive it. Such a gift, even from God, is completely worthless as long as it sits unopened on the doorstep of my life. He's always offered his light. It's only now that I've decided to receive it, to bring it inside my heart."

9

The Walk

Of all my favorite outdoor adventures, cross-country skiing ranks in the top three. I love the total body workout, the fact that you are not confined to a trail, and the overwhelming beauty of a winter-cloaked wilderness. Most of all, I love the solitude. I treasure the profound, soul-drenching quiet that Nordic skiing offers. Because of this deep passion, I've made it one of my delightful missions in life to teach my staff this beautiful sport.

Early in the season, Laurie and I went up to one of the best jumping-off points into the Cascade Wilderness. After parking my truck at the base of Tumalo Mountain, I helped Laurie gear up, and together we headed out across Dutchman Flat. I planned for us to traverse downward through an old-growth forest and make our way north to Todd Lake. We would then skirt its heavily frozen edge and return back up the mountain flank by another route. Since it had snowed the night before, all leftover tracks were now only vague depressions in the drifts of untouched white.

Laurie and I chugged along side by side and took advantage of the opportunity to catch up on each other's lives since our last conversation a week prior. We covered ranch operations, my public speaking trips, and our recent holiday travels.

"I'll break trail if you talk." I flashed my friend a Cheshire smile.

"Deal!" Laurie's speedy response verified that I was on the heavy lifting end of this trade. Laurie laughed like a girl who had just stolen my last piece of gum. She jumped into the even tracks behind me.

I glanced back at her. She was smiling, beautiful, natural. I slowed down to a stop and reached my gloved hand back for her. "I just love doing this with you."

She stretched her hand forward and held mine. Her voice was warm. "I love this time together too."

I set the pace, and stride for stride, Laurie breathed in rhythm behind me. We left the ease of flat land and entered the ancient forest. Then we wove through the trees in a serpentine fashion, making our way down the mountainside. "So, how's your Mia baby these days?"

"Well, it's official. My dog is teaching me far more than I could ever teach her. What a crazy journey this has been. I still shake my head at the fact that it has taken a sightless dog to show me that I was the one who was blind all along."

I jumped in. "Now you know it's true! I keep telling you God has a sense of humor!"

While she laughed, I followed up my statement. "In many ways, dogs really are smarter than people. I used to roll my eyes at statements like that until I realized that if the standard for comparison is nothing more than, say, forgiveness, it's a done deal! Dogs know how to forgive and keep on forgiving. Man! Here I am a grownup, and in this area I'm still learning."

Dogs know how to forgive and keep on forgiving.

Laurie had become the sighted, two-legged student of a blind, four-legged teacher. Because of this new reality, she began to see her dog with a fresh perspective. Day after day, she watched in wonder at just how much alike they were in their blindness.

Laurie found she favored autumn for her walks with Mia. They would often take a well-liked trail along one of the waterways pouring through Central Oregon. Cast under a heavy morning frost a few weeks earlier, all creation plunged even deeper into the rich and earthy radiance of fall. Sedges reveled in golden apparel. Mountain ash enticed all with its kaleidoscope of color. Willows called out to join in the celebration of another passing season. Just as we might blow a kiss to our beloved, so too was autumn giving one last farewell before departing into winter's rest.

On one of their daily walks, Laurie observed a pattern. Mia became so distracted that she would stray down a scent path and soon be far behind her master's strolling pace. This seemed to happen for the same reason: Mia stopped heeding her master's voice or presence. It wasn't because Mia didn't know or trust Laurie. Rather, she was diverted by the next new thing more captivating than her owner. She'd lag behind, nose to the ground, oblivious to her master's commands. Laurie watched with sadness as Mia moved down one trail after another, drawn by her own curiosity. *At least we're still sort of together,* she conceded. But Laurie's methodical steps carried her forward, while Mia's wandering steps carried her farther away.

Once the novelty of Mia's diversion wore off, she would realize that Laurie was no longer next to her. Gripped by panic,

Mia would run in frantic circles. Even though Laurie was still with her and still calling out directions, Mia's hysteria overwhelmed her.

"Mia," Laurie called, but her calm voice was not enough to soothe her dog.

Laurie walked back to her spinning dog, knelt down, and swept her into her arms. "You're safe, my sweet girl. It's okay, we're okay. Everything's all right." Mia nearly climbed inside her jacket, and Laurie pulled her close and held her until she quieted.

From then on, Laurie understood that when Mia's fear heightened into frenzy, she found no comfort in her owner's scent, sound, or gentle guidance. The only thing that calmed Mia during such an episode was the security of her master's arms.

At first, Laurie took great satisfaction in this tender process of reassurance. But after the third, fifth, tenth time, her joy eroded into raw irritation. When Laurie retraced one backward journey after another to collect her wayward dog, her impatience began to boil.

During one such frustrating march backward, Laurie fumed. Her throat burned with the desire to shout. *How many times are you going to move away from me and then freak out because you think I have left you? How many times will I have to walk back and scoop you up before you simply learn to walk with me?*

Her dog just didn't get it. She kept bringing the same hardship upon herself all over again. Once more, Laurie knelt and hugged Mia against her chest. Then the truth pierced Laurie's heart like a perfectly aimed arrow.

How many times will I have to walk back and scoop you up before you simply learn to walk with me?

God has been asking me those same questions!

Laurie saw how she had been running like her dog after every bright and shiny attraction. She too had been intent on experiencing the next new thing. She was the one who had willingly chosen to follow each fascinating temptation down one rabbit trail after another. And even though God was still with her, Laurie's wandering steps had carried her away from his side.

Once she strayed from God and his light, panic soon followed. For much of her life, Laurie had been circling, crying out to him for help. All the old questions would arise out of her darkened heart. *Where are you, God? Why can't I hear you? Why have you abandoned me?*

But God had been there all along. Like Mia, Laurie kept running past him. She was focused only on her present troubles, ignoring his voice and his presence. Unlike Laurie's limited patience with Mia, God's patience with her had lasted a lifetime.

God's quiet voice filled her heart. *I am right here with you. Still your heart, and you will hear my loving voice. Oh, my child, I would never abandon you. I will never leave you. I am as close to you as your breath. I will be with you forever.*

Laurie hugged her girl. Still encircled in her arms, Mia licked Laurie's chin. Her panting slowed into long, steady breaths.

—⁓—

"I mean, really!" I saw one of Laurie's ski poles swing to the side, and I turned around just in time to see her throw both of them straight out. "Throughout my life, every time I was confused, troubled, or lost in uncertainty, God always came for me, caught me in his arms, and held me close. Looking back now, I see that there was not a time in my life when I cried out to God and he didn't come for me."

> *I am right here with you. Still your heart, and you will hear* *my loving voice.*

Sliding to a stop, Laurie planted both of her poles and looked at me thoughtfully. "My sweet blind dog has helped me understand that in every sorrow, fear, and loneliness, whether I could see him or not, God has always been with me."

10

The Storm

Laurie and I glided down onto the shallow rim of the lake. I loved the view that lay before us. Todd Lake is long and narrow, and we had the privilege of standing on the south edge to look north over its entire frozen length. Cradled in a bowl at six thousand feet, the frozen tarn rested, bordered by a bowing forest of snow-laden trees. The high ridge that soared over the north shore was emblazoned by brilliant sunlight. So dazzling was the white crest that I squinted in response to the reflected radiance. I studied the masterpiece before me, not wishing to miss a single magnificent detail. Standing in such a kingdom of glorious beauty filled my soul with wonder, with peace, with thanksgiving. I took several deep breaths, drawing in the silent harmony.

Finally, succumbing to the need for words, I turned to Laurie. "Before we get started, there are a few things I need to share with you. For safety's sake, I normally don't ski on frozen water. Today, I'm going to make an exception since the banks are choked with fallen trees, and it would be a very slow trip if we attempted to ski around the lake through the tangle. I know this lake well, and the water frozen beneath us is less than two feet deep. If we were to break through, the combined depth of the ice and snow would not allow our skis to sink very far. Even though I believe it's deeply frozen, ice is funny stuff and should never be trusted in the wilderness. It's best never to ski on water, but if you must, only do so where you're certain that it's very shallow. Got it?"

"Got it!" Laurie emphasized her response with a decisive dip of her chin.

"Just a little tip from your Mama K."

We laughed at my use of this endearment. It was the name Laurie had given me months earlier.

"Hey, I love your Mama K tips! They help keep me informed and alive out here. That's a good thing! Alive is a good thing."

As our laughter trailed off, I could sense that Laurie needed to express something. I chose to stand fast and wait for her words to come.

Wondering what our next move would be, Laurie glanced over at me. Seeing my expression, she instantly dropped her gaze to her boots. I allowed my eyes to journey back over the lake and waited. Still staring downward, Laurie began to kick the snow off the surface of her skis.

Without looking up, she said, " 'Try again' has become one of the major themes of my life these days." She continued to pop snow up with her skis.

"I've always thought trying again was a good thing," I said. "You say that as if it's a bad thing. What's up with that?"

I motioned for her to come beside me so we could get underway. The rhythmic *swish, swish, swish* of our skis filled the air as we glided through the powdery snow that draped the edge of the lake. We covered nearly the entire length of the frozen body of water, and Laurie was still locked in a vise of wordlessness. I feared she had lost her nerve, so I finally stopped and stared at her with a coaxing smile.

She moaned in full recognition that I was not going to let her bow out.

I persisted in my silent prompt and raised my eyebrows in the universal position of "Well?"

"Oh man! I was hoping you wouldn't notice that I'm skipping this one."

"No such luck, Lou!" I swung my pole around and clinked it against hers. "You know I love you too much for that."

"Ohh-kay." Her big sigh let me know she was preparing herself to step across the awaiting threshold.

"Okay…okay…" she mumbled as if thumbing through her own thoughts. "Okay, so I wanted God to show me his light. I wanted my own relationship with him, remember?"

"I do remember."

"Even after making that decision, in honesty, I still wasn't committed—not to God, not to anything. I asked God to show me his light, to lead me, but I still wasn't relying on him. I knew that God could and even *wanted* to show me the way. And, in my head, I wanted it too, but in my heart and my actions, I still wanted my own way more. Deep inside, I knew my prayer to him hadn't been completely earnest. It was another coin tossed in the heavenly fountain—a token to make me feel better, not become better.

"Although I told myself that I wanted to follow God, I didn't want him bad enough to surrender my life to his leading. I prayed for God to lead me, yet nothing in my life, thoughts, or actions indicated that I actually wanted to follow him."

Laurie stopped talking.

I skied on in silence, hoping to create an empty stage for

Laurie to fill. Honest confrontations with oneself are often the most difficult confrontations of all. Moments passed, marked only by the soft sound of our skis gliding through the snow.

Laurie had retreated into the tracks behind me. From over my shoulder, I heard her clear her throat. "Every big and little thing that came my way still upset me, still completely derailed me. It was as if I was still looking for things to be angry about instead of looking for ways to resolve my problems. I had the opportunity to follow

Honest confrontations with oneself are often the most difficult confrontations of all.

God, to walk in his light. Yet I was still choosing to walk my own way, to live in my hurt, longing, and frustration. I was not at peace. I was still wrestling. Sad, really, because I could have chosen well. I just didn't.

"I was at home one night, waiting for my roommate to call me. We had made plans earlier to spend some time together. I waited hours for her to contact me. Throughout the evening, she didn't return any of my phone calls. She was completely blowing me off, and I assumed that she had chosen instead to spend the time with another friend she valued more than me. When I finally accepted the fact that she had rejected me, I was just so hurt, confused, and mad. In that moment, I knew that all my fears about being unaccepted by this world were con-firmed. In my broken state, I decided I was just done trying!"

—ᴍᴍ—

Feeling cast aside, Laurie loaded Mia into her car and started driving east. She headed toward one of the most desolate places she knew. She didn't want to see anyone. She just wanted to be alone. Driving through the night with Mia beside her, she had no destination, no plan, no agenda. Nothing filled her mind other than escape.

The night grew darker as Laurie drove away from civiliza-tion. Strong winds buffeted the High Desert. A blizzard was threatening. The full moon raced before the storm, dashing from a constant pursuit of clouds. Scattered snow blew across the road from the leading edge of the tempest.

Laurie knew there were no gas stations in this direction for nearly a hundred miles and drove as far as she dared. When she finally steered off the road and pulled her car to a stop, the full wrath of the storm had been unleashed. The turbulent weather escalated with Laurie's emotions into a tangle of confusion and chaos.

I'm not ready to turn back. I'm not ready to go home...to face my roommate...to face my life.

The power of the wind rocked Laurie's car. Inside, on the

seat beside her, Mia lay fast asleep. Laurie sat in silence. If someone were to have peered through the car window, they would
have seen that on the outside Laurie seemed peaceful, like the
dog sleeping beside her. But on
the inside, Laurie raged like the
storm howling around her.

On the inside, Laurie raged like the storm *howling around her.*

In that moment, the flimsy
layer of falsehood she'd chosen
to hide behind her entire life fi-
nally collapsed. Laurie's emotions came boiling out in a volcanic fury.

"I accused God! I spoke harshly to him. I blamed him for
all my failures. All that was wrong in my life, I shoved upon
him every hurtful thing that had ever happened to me. I didn't
stop for air. I just gushed out all that was burning in my soul
before God."

Laurie shouted, accused, and cried, purging all that was in
her heart. Twenty minutes later, her fiery rant ended. There was
nothing left to say. She had finally spoken the awful monsters
she had kept alive in her heart for years.

Exhausted and nauseous from her emotional outpouring,
Laurie sat in numb silence. Indignant, she waited for an answer from God. She looked up at the stormy night sky. Like a

celestial stampede, the wind-driven clouds raced across the moon. Leaning her left elbow on the window ledge, Laurie rested her head in her palm. She looked across at her sleeping dog, lying nose to tail in a soft circle of white hair. The storm outside and the rage inside hadn't disturbed Mia's slumber.

You're totally at peace in my presence, aren't you, girl? No matter what's going on around us, you still choose to rest. She reached over and ran her hand over Mia's brow.

Then a small but firm voice spiraled from beyond the storm into her soul. Words from the Bible streamed through her mind, words Laurie had read earlier that day. The verse told about the angels who circle God's throne and never cease worshiping him. Day and night they cry out, "Holy, holy, holy."[1]

The angels' only cry was to praise a holy God.

I've been crying out to God too, but my words have been far from holy. My words have been demanding, arrogant, selfish.

Laurie sat in hollow silence.

Slowly, a feeling blanketed her, an understanding, a warmth. She could sense comprehension filling her soul, a deep realization of just who it was she was addressing.

Her faults suddenly weighed heavily on her heart. What right did she have to bring accusations before a holy God? None. Even now, after her blistering outburst against him, all she felt in return was love. God's love poured over her, drenching her parched soul with complete acceptance of who she was.

He did not reject her; he did not scold her. He chose only to embrace her. Against such love, Laurie had no defense.

Overwhelmed, her heart broke. What she should be giving him was her thankfulness. Devastated by shame, guilt, and sorrow, Laurie was consumed by uncontrollable sobs. Her face dropped into her hands, and tears poured through her fingers.

She grieved for all her arrogance and accusatory pride that had somehow made her feel justified to stand against the God she claimed to serve. She cried over every self-appointed roadblock. She mourned for every obstacle she'd set before God so that she wouldn't have to live for him.

"God, you love me so completely despite these things," Laurie whispered.

For so many years, I thought I was good enough, as good as the next person. But the truth is, I am simply a broken sinner, bowing before a loving and holy God. The only thing I should be expressing to God is gratitude.

The storm outside raged on, but the storm in Laurie's heart began to subside. As her dog had already discovered, before a loving master, there is always a place to rest. Mia embodied what her master could also choose: peace.

Without a word, I stopped skiing and reached for my friend. There in the snow, on the north end of Todd Lake, we embraced. Laurie's body shook in silent remorse. After long moments of grieving, she began to rally. I released my friend and waited as she dried her face. During warmer months, this end of the lake was green and marshy, but now we stood in a meadow of pure white. One stunted, solitary tree knelt in the snow beside us. Bent under the weight of winter, it appeared to be praying for us. I smiled at the thought. Without a word, we began to stride once more.

True to her burgeoning courage, Laurie spoke again.

"I hadn't talked to God, really talked to him, in a long time." Her voice caught. "Earlier that day, when I read my Bible, it didn't mean much to me. I remember putting my Bible down and feeling frustrated that even when I tried spending time with God, when I tried to understand, when I tried to straighten things out in my life, God still let me down—how dare he!

"I had asked him to help me and show me his light; shouldn't he also make my life easier and more comfortable to bear? Since I had asked for his help, it didn't seem like anything in my life had changed at all. So where's the help? What's the point? What's the use?"

I looked back at Laurie and nodded slightly, letting her know I was with her, I was listening.

"So that night I drove out to the desert. The storm blew in, and I blew up…at God."

Her voice was so choked with emotion that I could barely hear her.

"Then, when I finally fell silent, God came through the darkness and met with me. He came not with anger, condemnation, or judgment, but in complete tenderness. That night, right then, right there, I confessed. I confessed out loud in the storm that I am no longer my god. Jesus is.

"The storm outside still raged, but the storm inside my life had been laid to rest. I finally decided to surrender. Even though I had spoken of it earlier in my life, I had never really done it. I had never honestly surrendered my life or my control of it."

I considered her statement. "Your control? Honestly, what do we control? When is the last time you told your heart to beat? Or your eyes to see? How often do we direct the rhythm of our breathing? The only thing we actually do control in this life is the ability to choose our attitude, our beliefs. The truth about our being 'in control' is that it is an illusion we want to believe is real."

Laurie nodded before adding, "I lived a long time convincing myself that my illusion of control was real, believing that I didn't really need God to lead me. As I said, I hadn't yet surrendered control of my life, my whole life, to God…not until that night."

I stopped skiing and looked at my friend. I wanted her to see my eyes, to see that they were full of tears, tears of joy for the hope she had found. For the hope she chose to receive, for the peaceful freedom that comes in knowing

The only thing we actually do control in this life is the ability to choose our attitude, our beliefs.

Christ. Laurie had struggled for so long. For years she had battled her internal storms; now my friend had chosen to finally step out of the tempest. She was done fighting. It was time to surrender, to embrace the peace that had always been available to her.

I wiped my eyes. "Wow, Lou, your whole life is about to change. I don't mean your circumstances. I don't mean that everything is suddenly going to be all hearts and roses. I mean that you are about to change, your heart, your attitude. Truly finding the peace of Christ is like finding the eye of the storm. The hurricane is still there, but because of what the Lord has done for us, we can abide in his peace through any storm."

Laurie smiled. I held my palm in front of her, and she responded with a glove-muffled high-five. While we were stopped, I decided to shed a layer.

Laurie used this moment to keep processing her thoughts out loud. "It was kinda like I was wandering in the desert and knew about the oasis; I just chose to never go there. Even though my heart was parched with thirst, when others led me to God, I still chose not to drink. Often I had stayed in the coolness, the beauty, the soothing presence of God, but I had never received the cup he offered me. Knowing about the water, even holding a full cup in my hands, still couldn't keep me from dying of thirst. I had to choose to receive the water, to drink it in. By the same token, it was not enough for me to simply know about God—I needed to receive him into every part of my life."

I planted my poles together, folded my hands over the grips, and rested my chin on top.

"When I was in my car surrounded by the storm," Laurie continued, "I stared at Mia lying beside me still sound asleep. She was at peace, resting in my presence. She was completely unruffled by the raging storm outside. She was with me, and that was enough for her. Without a word, my dog became the perfect example of how I should be with my God—I can choose to rest in him. No matter what storm may rage around me, I can rest in his presence."

"Oh, Lou. Let this image be the strong cord that binds you to the peace of Christ. You know where *your* choosing has led…now it's time for you to choose him to lead."

Laurie took a long, deep breath. "I know that Mia's life will still present challenges. So will mine. None of my problems were magically resolved that night, nor did any of my hardships instantly disappear. Something even better happened. I realized for the first time in my life that—like my sweet dog—I can rest peacefully in the presence of my Master."

Laurie maneuvered her skis close to mine. Her eyes were sparkling now. I was struck by the radiance that beamed out from them. It was the same brilliance I had just seen earlier, shimmering off the ridge top above us. I smiled in recognition. Both wonders came from the same source of beauty, hope, and peace.

"Through all we've discovered together, there's still one difference between my dog and me. Mia is still blind." Laurie paused as the tears welled up. "But I can see—really see—for the first time."

11

The Purpose
in Proximity

You know, because of Mia, I now understand that it's not possible for God's light, his truth, to fill the space within my heart that's already full of me."

Laurie reached across my kitchen counter and helped me gather up a gigantic bowl of salad, several bottles of dressing, and a large Crock-Pot full of pasta. A late fall breeze had been scattering leaves all afternoon. Now they swirled along my deck in a wordless dance of color.

It was Tuesday evening, and our Ranch Fellowship, a relaxed "cowboy church" in our barn, would be starting within the hour. To brace against the night's chill, we pulled on our jackets and headed out the door, our arms loaded with all the food we could carry. We chose our steps with caution in the mounting darkness, mindful not to slip. I noticed that Laurie needed to finish her thought, so I slowed my pace even further.

Laurie seized the opportunity. "I've squandered so much time as an adult struggling to become dependable, strong, and stable. You know, all the things you think will make you valuable to others. Yet instead of choosing to take the small, consistent steps to nurture those attributes, I've done nearly the opposite."

It's not possible for God's light, his truth, to fill the space within my heart that's already full of me.

"The opposite? What do you mean by that?"

"Oh, please don't get me wrong, I'm not saying that I have a grip on any of these things yet. What I am saying is, I now recognize that for much of my life I've been an impostor, a temporary look-alike that only gave the appearance of having those admirable qualities. When all along, the truth was I had none of them."

Laurie juggled the food items over to her left arm and pushed open the gate that leads out of our front yard and down the grassy hill toward the barn.

"If I'm brutally honest with myself, until recently I've never worked long enough or hard enough to earn any of those worthy characteristics. I applied only enough effort to look like I had them." Self-directed disdain tinged her voice. "Candidly, I'd have to admit that my greatest accomplishment of late was to maintain the facade of my former ways. I've been an actor for so long."

She shook her head. "I saw this same pretense reflected by my dog during our trip to the coast. Mia was fine as long as she paid attention to my voice and followed my commands. But as soon as she stopped listening to me and started behaving like she knew what to do and already knew the way, her life quickly became very uncomfortable. I've done that too. I've pretended like I was close to God, following his voice, but my life, my actions, proved otherwise. Even though I said I was close to him, I wasn't.

"Once again, it's my precious little blind dog who's shown me that the real problem with faking you know something is that you actually don't know it when you need it the most. Knowing I should have a close relationship with God is not the same as pursuing it. Mia has shown me that if you're going to purpose to know someone, you can't do it from a distance.

The real problem with faking you know something is that you actually don't know it when you need it the most.

"A few weeks ago, during one of our fellowships, something happened between Mia and me, something that has moved me to seek change in my own life."

—⁂—

Laurie walked up the hill with Mia in tow and arrived at the main barn moments before the Ranch Fellowship began. Kids, families, staff, volunteers, and friends of all ages were invited to this twice-monthly event. The seasonal ebb and flow of folks coming typically ranges from around one hundred fifty people in the winter months to over three hundred fifty during the summer. On this night, the crowd looked to be somewhere in between.

Laurie loved this gathering. One of the things she appreciated most was the diversity of the group. Families of all ages and financial brackets, single parents, college students, and widows all mingled together in a congenial time of togetherness. Some folks came to rest and indulge in the alternating catered or potluck meal, some came for the unabashed singing, others came for the encouragement. Many came just for the sense of walking into a giant family and knowing they belonged. No matter what drew people to the Ranch Fellowship, it was clearly one of the most beloved events at Crystal Peaks.

Escaping the nippy night air, Laurie and her dog bumped through the crowded doorway and into the barn. Mia was beset by a horde of little hands that wished to greet her. Laurie scanned the packed room, only to be met by a swarm of grinning, grubby kids. They ignored the evening chill and rushed to grab her hands and lead her outside toward their favorite horse and to show her how they could roll without stopping all the way down the grassy hill.

Once Laurie made her way back to the barn, she was met by five-year-old Kendal, who held her arms high and jumped. Laurie caught and balanced the little girl on her hip. Before she could take another step, the tiny arms of Kendal's friend also reached up for some love. Laurie knelt and opened her arms to receive them both in a jubilant group hug. Whether she had been working in the ranch office or out in the arena, no long or exhausting day ever dampened her desire to come to the Ranch Fellowship.

During the summer months, this hospitable gathering was always held outside on a grassy hill. But once the temperature began to drop, the Fellowship moved indoors into the relative comfort of the barn. A massive wood stove against the north wall churned out home-style comfort, inviting all to enjoy its hearty embrace. The rustic conditions provided the perfect setting for Mia to come with Laurie and sit in on the fun.

Winter coats lay piled on benches. Bowls and platters competed for space on the serving counters. Soon dirty plates, napkins, and cups, along with food remnants, would lay scattered across a dozen large wooden tables, all giving testimony to a meal well savored.

Laurie watched a group of small boys crowded around the dessert table. They appeared as innocent as cherubs and as subtle as a pack of wolves, and their mischievous grins belied their intentions. They checked the crowd to see if their mothers were watching and then stole glorious finger swipes of frosting off a tray of cupcakes. Each giggling victory made Laurie laugh too.

The crowd of voices lifted in disjoined volume like a grade school band practice. Laurie knew that trying to guide Mia through such loud surroundings with voice commands was going to be impossible. To lead her dog through the din, Laurie hooked Mia's collar with a single finger.

Once the hearty meal and equally hearty singing concluded, the crowded barn quieted as Troy endeavored to teach about trust. He started by sharing a wild adventure he had experienced while learning how to pilot a plane. Many of the same little boys who were earlier embezzling frosting now sat on the floor at Troy's feet, completely spellbound. Minutes into Troy's talk, Kendal tugged on Laurie's sleeve and whispered, "I have to go to the bathroom!"

Laurie looked for the least disruptive path out of the barn. Bending low, she led Kendal with one hand and Mia with the other. In her urgency, Kendal pulled Laurie so fast that Mia couldn't step around the obstacles she couldn't see. Laurie lost her grip on Mia's collar in the rush to the door and quickly backtracked to retrieve her sightless friend. Not wishing to disturb others more than she already had, Laurie chose not to verbally guide her dog. Instead, she used the only thing she could think of: she snapped her fingers by Mia's head. When her dog turned toward the sound, Laurie rubbed Mia's brow. Laurie repeated this process until Mia understood that when she followed the sound of the snaps, she was rewarded with love.

Mia was a quick learner. In just moments, Laurie was leading Kendal with one hand and snapping for her dog with the other. Mia stayed close to her master and followed the sound of Laurie's snapping fingers all the way to the outhouse. Laurie marveled at how rapidly Mia understood that there were times when she needed to be extra attentive and close to Laurie. It was no longer her master's voice that Mia followed—it was her actions.

If you're honestly going to follow another, you can't do it from a distance.

Born out of those quiet interactions, a new season of deeper communication grew between woman and dog. Mia discerned that there were times when following Laurie's words was not enough. When Laurie moved in silence, Mia would trace her steps by keeping the tip of her nose in contact with the outside of her master's calf. When Laurie stopped, Mia stopped. When Laurie moved forward, Mia moved forward. When Laurie sat down, Mia would lie at her feet and rest either her chin or her front paw on top of her owner's foot.

Mia's sense of her master's nearness only sharpened with time. Her perceptiveness is what prevented her from ever losing the one she loved. When Mia was in close contact with Laurie, voice commands were no longer necessary. Her dog stayed so close that she followed not only her master's voice, but also her very movements.

Her dog's actions made it clear. If you're honestly going to follow another, you can't do it from a distance. There is great purpose in proximity.

—⁓—

Inside the barn, we unloaded the food and arranged the dishes on the potluck table.

Laurie continued to voice her reflections. "It was my dog once again who modeled the truth that if I'm going to know and follow someone I love, it makes little sense to try and accomplish that if there's a huge gap between us. To truly imitate the movements of another, I need to mirror them as closely as possible. My dog has taught me that it is indeed doable to know someone you can't see with your eyes. Just like when I rise, she rises. When I move my foot, she moves with it. She has shown me how to stop, rest, and move however and wherever her master does. My dog has chosen to mirror me without hesitation, without ever questioning why."

"Keep going! I love this example."

In her rising enthusiasm, Laurie gained more steam. "If I'm ever going to become honestly strong, dependable, and stable, I first need to empty the fake junk that previously filled my life and allow myself to become weak and dependent in an effort to build what is real. Do you see what I'm saying?"

"Yup, more than you know." I moved over to an empty table closer to the wood stove. Patting the bench with my hand, I motioned for Laurie to come and sit with me. "Lou, the fact is, strength doesn't come from strength—it grows out of our weakness. For us to become dependable, we first have to walk through the process of being truly dependent. Does that make sense?" I asked.

Laurie nodded as she stared at the fire. "I have to go back to the basics. I need to let go of what I once believed was right—my way—and quit pretending to know things I don't. I want to follow not only my master's voice, but his actions as well. Like my dog, only I can determine to shift myself closer to the peace that comes when I move silently with my master. It's within his presence that I find complete rest. In this perfect place of greatest dependence, I need no words at all."

12

The Gift of Joy

From atop my trusted horse, Ele, I looked over at Laurie, mounted on Lightfoot, a gray Arabian gelding. Lightfoot is the most balanced combination of what I like to call "gentle fire"—he'd become one of our most beloved horses on the ranch. The ease with which Laurie sat on him divulged that they were dear friends. Laurie's dark blue helmet drew out and deepened the color of her eyes, already framed by her sweeping eyelashes. The combination was simply lovely.

Many years ago, my precious grandmother taught me that kind thoughts are wasted if they don't become kind words. "Wow! You look beautiful today."

Laurie's eyebrows shot up in surprise. She laughed and gestured toward her faded, threadbare jeans. "Yeah, I'm pretty stylish, all right."

"No, I'm not talking about your clothes, I'm talking about you. You look happy, and you seem content."

"Maybe it's because I'm learning how to be. Mia keeps teaching me one life lesson after another. My dog has not only become one of my most cherished friends and companions, she's also a mentor to me. Can you believe it?" She smiled, really smiled.

Happiness is a choice; it's not something that just happens to people.

I nodded. I could believe it. God has used animals in my own life to heal so much. I let my friend's words hang in the cool afternoon air. Our horses took us down one of our favorite dusty trails.

"What is Mia teaching you as your mentor?"

"Well, I'm learning through the actions of my dog that happiness is a choice; it's not something that just happens to people. I'm responsible to choose it—not wait for it to choose me. I heard recently that happiness is based on our outward circumstances, but joy—real joy—comes from the inside, from God."

Laurie shifted in her saddle and looked at me. She started

to laugh at what she was about to say. "Mia's like a superhero. She models qualities I can only hope to acquire someday."

I joined Laurie's laughter at the image of her dog being a superhero. "Hmm, somehow the cape and tights thing just doesn't seem to suit her. But then again, I don't know Mia as well as you do."

Laurie kept laughing. It was a genuine sound that far outweighed my dumb joke.

"So what's your superdog motivating you to aspire toward?"

Thinking, Laurie rested her hand on Lightfoot's withers, as if confirming his steadiness. "It wasn't until Mia arrived in my home that I began to understand just how much I have lived my life guided solely by my emotions."

"Guided by your emotions? Yikes! Now there's some mean quicksand waiting to swallow you whole!" I laughed.

"No, really, I was like a dried-up autumn leaf. I allowed myself to be driven by the wind, never really knowing how or why I felt the way I did. Every little gust of life would toss me up or down in a whirlwind of emotional drama."

Laurie laid the back of her hand across her helmeted brow. "Drama, drama, drama! I was all about the drama."

I laughed again and urged my horse to slow a bit so we could remain side by side as we walked down the trail. "Well, girl, I'd say that you've enjoyed some fine company. There isn't a woman alive who—if she's honest with herself—hasn't stepped out onto the drama stage from time to time."

Laurie was still laughing. "I know, but if they ever had a leader, I'm sure I would've been their exalted queen!" She extended her fingers above her helmet to form an impromptu crown and declared, "You know, 'Hail to the queen!'"

"Hail to the queen!" I echoed, raising my fist in the air. I immediately withdrew my salute. "No, wait! If I were playing the drama game, I wouldn't salute you! I'd start to cry and say, 'You hurt my feelings! I can't worship Your Highness because *I'm* the queen!' I'd rather go somewhere and be depressed and dive into a bucket of ice cream to soothe my bruised ego."

Laurie raised her index finger. "Make that a bucket of mint chocolate chip for me!" Cracking up over our fun exchange, we rode on into the fragrant juniper forest.

"I wish being a drama queen were actually this fun, but it's not. When I did that—the drama thing—I felt miserable inside. I chose to live my life at the complete mercy of my latest emotion. It took Mia to help me understand that whatever emotion I yielded to became my master. I had chosen to become a slave to how I felt."

Laurie reached down and gently rubbed Lightfoot's smooth neck. "By allowing myself to be carried by every restless wave in the sea of my emotions, I always lived in a very unstable place. Nothing was ever my fault. Everything always 'just happened' to me. Therefore, I could play the role of a victim who had no responsibility to change.

"Looking back, I can see how I talked myself into believing that I was helpless to control how I felt. As long as I kept choosing to base my happiness on temporary things—guess what? My happiness would be just as temporary. Sadly, mine was."

She fell silent. I wondered if the rhythm of Laurie's horse beneath her was as comforting as my horse was to me. I couldn't recall a moment in my life when being in the saddle on the back of a dear friend wasn't time well spent. The reassuring cadence always persuaded my heart to relax, to release the hurt I held inside. To express my gratitude, I reached back and rubbed the top of my mare's powerful rump.

When Laurie spoke again, I could hear her voice strengthen with a new determination. "Unlike me, my dog has lost nearly everything—except her joy. There have been countless times when I've been so wrapped up in my dumb stuff, so anxious and upset over the difficult things that have come my way. Yet Mia has allowed no person, veterinarian, or circumstance to steal her joy. In the brief season I've known my girl, she's persevered through more painful obstacles and suffering than I have yet to know in my lifetime."

Falling silent again, Laurie glanced out into the forest. Emotion tightened her voice as she recounted her dog's losses, her pain.

Mia had lived under a rusted-out car.

She had been starved by her previous owners, which had caused her to lose over half her normal weight.

Diabetes had devastated her body, threatening her life.

She had put up with a vet who had extracted only half of a tooth, resulting in a painful, feverish infection.

Mia had undergone more than a dozen veterinary procedures and surgeries.

She had lost several of her teeth, her reproductive organs, an eye, and her sight.

She had suffered the loss of her original home, her health, and her independence.

Daily, she tolerates several insulin injections.

Frequently she crashes into something, painfully splitting her lip or bloodying her nose.

Your little blind dog really is a superhero.

After Laurie had recited the list of Mia's trials, her eyes met mine. "Mia didn't choose for any of that to happen; it just did. The most amazing thing to me is, Mia's happy! Through all her adversity, she remains joyful. Despite her hardships, she still wags her whole body at the simple thrill of hearing my voice."

"Wow, to consistently choose joy no matter what befalls us—that is actually something to aspire to. You were right. Your little blind dog really is a superhero."

Thumb pointing at her chest, Laurie said, "No matter what emotions surface, I'm the only one responsible for how I react to them. So as long as I keep choosing to be controlled by my feelings of anxiety, sadness, depression, anger, or bitterness, I don't get to blame anyone but myself. Since I alone select how I feel, I can't complain about something that I can choose to change every moment of every day!"

I drew and pointed both of my hands toward her like pistols. "Yes, yes, yes! That's it! Now there's the truth!"

"I know it's the truth; I do know it. I just can't help thinking about how dense I've been all these years. How sad and ridiculous that I blamed everything and everyone for my sorrows—except the one who was truly at fault. Me."

Laurie lengthened Lightfoot's reins, urging him to keep pace with my taller, faster horse. I noticed her effort and eased Ele back a little so Laurie could finish her thought.

"Mia has proved with her life that my current difficult circumstances aren't nearly as important as what I decide to do with them. How I act in these challenging situations determines who I really am and what I really believe. When I view my life from that perspective, it's far easier for me to focus on what I should do instead of on what I think I should have.

"I can either focus on complaining about my hardships or I can decide to allow each challenge to help me grow up. I think it's ironic that it took an animal, my little dog, to teach me how to behave, how to take responsibility for how I feel.

Circumstances don't dictate how I feel—I do.

"Although it might take me a lifetime to put into practice, because of Mia, I now understand that circumstances don't dictate how I feel—I do. I can always choose my attitude. I can always choose joy."

13

The Bridge of Trust

Our horses knew the direction we had just turned would lead them back to the grassy hill on the ranch, their favorite spot to graze. With a slope of green waiting, Ele and Lightfoot spontaneously picked up the pace. Swords of light sliced through the patchy clouds overhead, fending off the dissipating storm. Laurie turned her face toward the beams. "Wow, this place we get to live in, it's really something extraordinary.

"Hey, Mama K? You know what else is extraordinary? Mia lives her life in a way that proclaims the grass *isn't* greener on the other side—it's greener where you water it! It's greener where contentment flows. She reminds us to stop wishing for what we don't have and start caring for what we do! My little dog has taught me how much less energy it takes to rejoice in what I do have than to be resentful about what I don't.

"It's funny how when we choose joy, our problems don't go away, but our sorrow, loneliness, and low self-esteem do. I want to choose to look beyond my own troubles and, instead, choose to help others through theirs. I wish to experience daily joy like that. Between Mia's example and what God has done in my life, I now know that I can."

I looked at Laurie. "I think it's incredible that your dog, the same one who used to live under a rusty car, taught you all that."

With near blinding in-

When we choose joy, our problems don't go away, but our sorrow, loneliness, and low self-esteem do.

tensity, the sun burst through again. This time, the thinning clouds were powerless to stop the growing brightness of its glory. Imitating sunflowers, Laurie and I turned our faces up toward the sun's brilliance. On this chilly day, we reveled in its warmth.

Laurie looked my way and tossed me a smile. "And it's not just me; she's teaching others too."

—ᴍ—

The first time I met Shelly, two things captured my attention. Her tall, slender build matched the hollow grief etched in her narrow face. She was a woman who bore much sorrow, and her countenance gave evidence of that fact. Coupled with her obvious heartache was her determination—even desperation— to do whatever it took to help her children. If I knew nothing more about her, that was enough to gain my compassion and my wholehearted desire to assist her.

Shelly came to the ranch for help, and like many other single mothers, she resembled a female Atlas, bending low under her crushing burdens. As if shouldering the weight of a master's program wasn't enough, she was also battling cancer and struggling through a vicious divorce. Because of the marital chaos, she was the sole provider for her twelve-year-old twins. Her arduous load spilled onto her son, Kent, who had tumbled into a black chasm of despondency. An equally ugly toll was being exacted on his sister, Anna, who was plagued by crippling shyness and low self-esteem. Exhausted, sick, and alone, the young mother reached out to the ranch for help.

In return, Laurie reached back and offered to mentor Anna weekly. To help the willowy little girl gain confidence, the two of them worked to train a beautiful but dominant horse named Starbuck. In doing so, Anna needed to be gentle, consistent, and assertive. She had to set boundaries with Starbuck and enforce them. In a short amount of time, Anna came to deeply love the roan-buckskin gelding that challenged her to be strong.

Slowly, she emerged from her dark place like a fawn stepping into a clearing for the first time.

Although invited often by his mother and sister, Kent refused to have anything to do with the ranch. He didn't want to interact with any of the horses or staff. Instead, he stayed in the backseat of the family car parked at the bottom of the hill. He sat and waited for hours, staring at nothing but his feet on the floorboards. Bound by an armor of reclusiveness, Kent remained alone.

On a day when Anna's mom drove into the ranch yard to pick her up, Laurie met Kent for the first time. She leaned down to look into the car and greeted him. "Hi, Kent. It's nice to finally meet you."

He wouldn't look up. He wouldn't speak. He never gave any indication that he even saw her.

Undeterred, Laurie said, "Hey, on Thursday afternoon we have a roundup. Everyone's welcome. We play games so crazy, you wouldn't believe it if I told you. It's so fun! I'd love for you to come and join us."

His silence and aversion to all eye contact told Laurie not to push him. Respectfully, she didn't.

From that point on, every encounter Laurie had with Kent was the same: no eye contact, no verbal communication, and no breakthrough. No matter how many times she tried, Laurie couldn't crack his shell of isolation. Nothing she did or said affected his withdrawn behavior.

Winter had tightened its grip on the High Desert when the twins' mother called Laurie to ask a favor. She needed to travel to Portland, a three-hour drive up and over the Cascade Divide, for a series of appointments and treatments for her cancer. Although the route is incredibly scenic during summer, in winter the road becomes treacherous, with violent storms. The combination of a dangerous drive and a daunting treatment compelled Shelly to ask for help. Her request was straightforward. "Will you take care of my children while I'm gone?"

"Yes, of course!" Laurie welcomed the opportunity to spend more time with this overburdened family she'd grown to love. She hoped that prolonged time with the twins would be the mortar that would bond them. Perhaps this would be the opportunity for her to gain access to Kent's heart.

Laurie drove over to the twins' home and received a few last-minute instructions from Shelly. After a quick hug goodbye, Laurie turned her full attention to the kids. Now that she was in Kent's house, his avoidance morphed into a different but equally distant form. He sequestered himself upstairs in his room, spending time only in the company of his computer. Staunch in his decision to stay disconnected, he refused to eat dinner that night with Laurie and Anna. Instead, he crept downstairs later to get a snack.

"Hey, Kent, can I help you with some dinner?" Laurie asked.

No answer. With a cache of food tucked under his arm, he scuttled out of the kitchen as quickly as he had come.

Kent stumbled across one obstacle in his avoidance maneuver: Mia lying on the stairs. Her chosen place to recline blocked his escape route. Each time he passed, Mia looked up in the direction of his face.

For reasons known only to Kent, this simple action derailed his retreat to his room. Stopping, Kent looked down at Mia, perhaps staring at her blindness, her weakness. He knelt on the stair next to the sightless dog and studied her in the stillness. As if pulled by an unseen force, his hand moved toward her, and he gently stroked her back. Laurie watched from her vantage point and witnessed the unfolding of an answer to her prayer. Mia, without fanfare, began to dismantle Kent's defensive armor.

Mia, without fanfare, began to dismantle Kent's defensive armor.

Like a timid mouse stealing out of the darkness for crumbs,

Kent made hushed sojourns down the stairs to find Mia. Each visit was the same. Kent soundlessly emerged from the shadows, knelt beside Mia to run his hand across the top of her head, and then disappeared back into the darkness.

The full impact Mia had had on Kent's heart wasn't revealed until several weeks later. Shelly again asked Laurie to spend the afternoon with the twins while she worked to meet a thesis deadline. In an effort to get the kids out of the house, to move, to breathe fresh air, Laurie offered to take them to Tumalo Reservoir. Anna's grin gave her answer, but Kent averted his eyes, as usual, and wouldn't respond to her invitation.

Laurie told him, "Mia's waiting in the car. She's coming with us."

Kent looked out the window, trying to see Mia. He disappeared for a moment and then reappeared, with the obvious addition of a jacket. He brushed passed Laurie without a glance and climbed into the backseat of her Olds Bravada, next to Mia.

Once at the reservoir, Laurie instructed the kids to do silly things so she could photograph them and tape up the resulting pictures around their home in an attempt to cheer up their mom. Given permission to goof off, the twins jumped over sage, made silly faces, and performed wobbly cartwheels. Mia also joined in on the fun. In a version of canine tag, Mia would run ahead of the kids and then bound back to them. She would wiggle nose to tail and jump around them in crazy leaps and then run ahead again. Anna and Kent delighted in Mia's playing with them. Every time she circled the twins with her antics, Anna couldn't contain her laughter.

Laurie was grateful that Kent seemed to be having fun even though he scarcely acknowledged her. Throughout the day, he remained determined not to look at her. It was clear that he was still uncomfortable with her and didn't like it when she directed questions his way. Choosing not to force a friendship, Laurie allowed the day to simply unfold. She hoped all their comical behavior would shake Kent loose and help him relax in her presence.

When the sun dipped low, the temperature followed. The kids raced back with Mia to Laurie's car and dove into its relative shelter before the cold could follow them. Laurie could hear muffled commotion from the backseat. She glanced up in her rearview mirror and saw Kent guiding Mia to sit next to him. Laurie smiled; her dog could go where she could not. Brick by brick, Mia was building a foundation of trust in Kent's heart.

Laurie drove the kids home and took them inside. She listened with delight as Anna recounted their adventures to Shelly. Laurie was uncertain of the impact of the day on Kent until she said it was time for her to go.

Kent's strong response surprised Laurie. He suddenly turned toward her and cried, "No!"

He ran past Laurie to Mia and quickly went down on his knees and hugged her with a tender squeeze. Looking only at Mia, he said, "I'm not ready for you to go yet."

Then he did it. With eyebrows pressed together—pleading—Kent turned and looked directly at Laurie. For the first time ever.

Laurie couldn't hold inside what brimmed over in her heart; she smiled at him. And then, almost imperceptibly, the corners of his mouth turned up in response. Kent smiled back. In that instant, a fragile bridge of trust spanned the distance between them. A bridge of trust…that Mia had built.

—⁓—

"Kim, I had been trying for months, but Mia did it! My little blind dog was the one who saw the way into that boy's closed heart. She opened the door of friendship between Kent and me. He's a completely changed boy! When I take Mia over for a visit, the moment he sees her, his face lights up with joy. Then he drops to one knee and lets her lick his entire face! I'm not sure whether to rejoice with him or gag for him. It's the sweetest, grossest thing!" She laughed at the mental image. "Yet Kent doesn't seem to mind a bit."

Who would have thought a blind dog could reach into a boy's prison and love him back to life?

I shook my head in acknowledgment. "Sweet Mia. How remarkable that your lovable, blind, bad-breath dog could go where no one else was allowed."

Laurie nodded. "It's incredible to me that Mia has unlocked Kent's heart. He's so much more alive with her than he's ever been with me. Because of Mia, he's a totally different kid now. Last week he came out to the ranch and loved it! His mom told me that he's been begging her to bring him back."

I slowed my horse and nudged her to sidestep over toward Lightfoot. I reached my hand out toward Laurie. She caught it and held on in a thoughtful moment. Releasing her hand, I looked at Laurie. "What a privilege it is to watch you become less of a receiver and more of a giver. I'm so deeply proud of you, Lou. In the few years I've known you, you've grown so much. *You're* the one who's the different kid now."

Who would have thought a blind dog could reach into a boy's prison and love him back to life?

14

The Closet

My heart was so full I couldn't help but laugh out loud. I looked over at Laurie. "Want to make a great day even better?" By shifting my eyes between Lightfoot and Ele, I made my message clear.

Laurie shot back an enthusiastic "You bet!" Together we seized the moment and galloped our horses with abandon down a forgotten dirt road. Cutting corners, we ducked under tree branches, dodged fallen logs, and jumped over rain runoff channels.

"Yeah!" I shouted over my shoulder as we thundered toward the direction of home, a half-dozen miles away. We approached the base of a steep incline and coaxed our energized horses down into a fast walk. When we neared the bottom of the hill, I gave quick instructions to Laurie. "Reach halfway up Lightfoot's neck and grab a handful of mane. I want you to lean forward and stand up in the stirrups and let him do his job. We'll go first to show you what I mean."

Like a four-legged freight train, Ele bounded up the hill in a series of powerful leaps. Once we reached the top of the ridge, I sat back down in my saddle. I dropped my reins and lowered my hands to rub both sides of my mare's neck in appreciation of a job well done.

From below, Laurie encouraged Lightfoot, and her voice carried up to me. "Good boy, good boy! You're amazing!" In an instant they popped over the top as if it were little more than a speed bump.

"Arabians! What's not to love?" I called out in pure admiration.

Once on top of the crest, we picked our way through a jumble of black lava rock. While our horses walked head to tail, I pointed out the panoramic view to the east. Geology intrigues me, so I took the moment to explain to Laurie how we were actually riding on the high side of a fault plane.

"All of Central Oregon is volcanic in origin and has been shaped by unique forces. See those black outcroppings of rock? They're the terminuses, the ends of some very old lava flows, which are primarily basalt, one of the heaviest stones on earth."

Laurie, who was still riding behind me, was silent. I wondered if I was boring her with my impromptu geology babble and swung around in my saddle to check on her.

She smiled at me and then glanced in the direction of the lava features I had just pointed out. Her expression was pensive, telling me that although she was looking at the phenomenon, she was not really seeing it. I could tell her mind was wandering, instead, in a wilderness of consideration.

Without thought, I slowed my horse's pace. "What is it?"

A surge of sadness clouded Laurie's eyes. "I just want to be there for her, you know? The road that awaits Mia is going to be far less kind than what she's already been through." Laurie's voice caught as her expression began to crumple.

I asked Ele to halt. Lightfoot sensed what he needed to do and stopped at my mare's shoulder. "Oh, Lou, you've given Mia such a wonderful end to her life. No matter what might lie ahead, she's secure in the loving home you've given her. Because of you, she'll know nothing but love right up until the very end. And that, my sweet girl, is a good end."

Laurie's gaze did not return to mine. Still looking away, she fought to control her emotions.

I held my horse steady next to Lightfoot. "You know that Dr. Shawn and I are friends, right?"

She sniffed and then nodded.

"He's told me more than once how incredibly fortunate Mia is that you adopted her. She would've died long ago had you not intervened. He also said he knows of few others who would've done what you're doing for Mia. He told me that nobody could do better for her than you have."

She raised one hand to her face and wept.

There, on top of a windswept ridge, two horses stood close to bear their riders even closer. A cold wind blew around us. I pulled up my fleece collar and buttoned my black Carhartt coat around it. It was hard to see my friend's heart break. Both of us knew that when Mia's time came, it would be a very difficult good-bye.

Laurie pulled one of her sleeves from under her coat and dried her eyes. She drew several deep breaths before she spoke again. "I feel like my whole life has been so mixed up, so about me. And then Mia came. In her unique way, she has helped me to see that my life is like a puzzle. Each piece by itself is confusing, but when fitted together into the bigger picture, there's a greater purpose. I can see that in my lame attempt to insulate myself from pain, I've also unintentionally isolated myself from really knowing love. In my need for self-protection, I've pulled so far back from anything that could emotionally challenge me to grow that I compromised growing altogether."

Laurie worked to push her damp sleeve back up under her

coat. "I didn't realize just how shut down I'd become until a little blind dog demonstrated how much more satisfying it is to live an honest and open life."

We started down the trail again. "I'm happy…" I spoke over my shoulder. "Girl, I'm so happy at how Mia's helping you to open up. As you already know, a closed heart only knows loneliness. It takes an open heart to receive gifts like hope and love, peace and joy."

"You're right," she said from behind me. "What I'm starting to grasp for the first time is that love doesn't just come in; we choose to let it in. Letting love in is now something that I'm working on. I need to choose to let love in."

A little blind dog demonstrated how much more satisfying it is to live an honest and open life.

I turned in my saddle to look back at Laurie. Her expression made me think she was mentally putting up a Post-it note with that same message across her heart. Note to self: *let love in!*

She gave me a weak smile. "It's the funniest thing. Issues I've tripped over most of my life, while spinning around in confusion, my dog does naturally. Experiencing things like love, peace, and joy aren't hard for her at all. I think love is so complex, yet my dog demonstrates that it can also be simple. Mia constantly shows me how easy it is to fill one's life with what actually matters, like being content with what you have. I've struggled with being content, but my dog hasn't. For her, contentment is effortless. I want to be like that. I want to have that same peaceful awareness.

"Almost every day she proves how things like sprawling in the sun can be one of the greatest treasures there is. I love it when Mia is resting outside in the yard. I can see her turning her head to catch the sound of the wind moving through the trees.

"Sometimes I see her tip her head completely sideways when she hears a favorite word, like *walk*. Maybe the greatest insight of all her dog wisdom is, if you love someone, let them know. There's no time like the present for a well-placed lick on the chin."

Laurie snickered. "Because of a dog, I now understand that a sincere kiss, no matter how stinky, is more valuable than gold."

—◊◊—

Mia's days were numbered.

That painful fact spurred Laurie to live more in the moment. Without trying, Mia challenged her master to make every ounce of time count, really count. Laurie understood that any day she and her dog spent together could be their last.

Late one afternoon, Laurie noticed that Mia didn't seem quite right. Laurie tried to soothe her mild concern by telling herself that her dog had just had a busy day and was probably tired. But Mia's odd behavior continued into the evening; she grew more and more restless. Instead of lying quietly next to Laurie's feet, Mia constantly shifted her weight, often getting up and roaming around the house. Laurie took her outside a few times, thinking maybe she was going to be sick, but the strange searching behavior only continued outdoors.

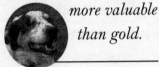

A sincere kiss, no matter how stinky, is more valuable than gold.

Laurie checked and rechecked Mia's medication schedule. *Okay, everything is fine with her meds. I didn't miss anything. I know she hasn't eaten anything she shouldn't have. Her amount of exercise hasn't varied much. She should be fine.*

By the time Laurie was getting ready for bed, Mia was nowhere to be found. An anxious search revealed that she had crawled into the back of Laurie's small closet. Mia had never re-moved herself like this before. "Oh, girl, what's going on? This isn't where you belong. What are you trying to tell me?"

Laurie had owned a dog in her youth and understood that a setting of privacy would probably herald how Mia would choose to leave this life. Dogs possess a sense of their own end and often will hide away from those they love when the time comes. Laurie refused to accept that possibility. She didn't want it to be true, not today.

Laurie pushed open the closet door a bit wider and sat down on the tan carpet next to Mia. She stroked her dog's lowered head and whispered her agony. "It can't be time, Mia. Not now. You're doing so well. Please don't go. Please don't leave."

Mia didn't stir, didn't have the energy even to respond. Her tail, which normally wagged behind her, now lay limp on the floor.

Laurie spoke again to Mia in whispers. "Come on, girl. Come with me."

Still no response. Her one remaining eye focused on nothing.

Laurie tried a different tactic. "Come on, Mia. It's time to go to bed." She crawled out of the closet, hoping Mia would follow as she always had.

Mia hesitated, then rallied herself. Step by slow step, she followed Laurie out of the closet and found her place on the plush oval dog pillow beside Laurie's bed. That is where she had slept nearly every night since she and Laurie had been together.

Laurie lay on the floor, her arms around her dog, assuring Mia of her love. After Mia settled into sleep, Laurie went back into the bathroom to finish her preparations for bed.

When Laurie returned to the bedroom, the dog bed was empty. Mia was gone.

She had retreated back into the closet. This time Mia had curled up in an incredibly small place in the very back corner. "Please, Mia, please... Please come."

But Mia didn't respond.

Laurie collapsed under the weight of her sorrow. "No, Mia. No, not now, not yet." She ran her hand over her dog's soft coat.

"I'm not ready to say good-bye." She laid her head on Mia's warm body. "Please, please don't go."

Laurie started to crawl away, begging Mia to follow, but this time her dog couldn't oblige her.

Mia was no longer able to crawl out to Laurie...so Laurie crawled in to her. Together they lay in the corner of the closet— a broken dog cradled in the arms of a broken girl.

"My little dog... You'll always be my little blind dog."

At first, Laurie wanted to encourage Mia to fight for her life. Yet on the heels of that yearning came an even stronger desire. It was her greater hope that the companion she loved so much wouldn't suffer.

Who am I to determine what should happen? Mia is the only one who can make that choice—to fight for more time or to let go. It's not my decision—it is Mia's.

If this was going to be her beloved dog's final night, Laurie wanted her to understand that she was cherished right up to the very end. She wanted Mia to know that she was loved and treasured, that her example of life had changed Laurie's outlook. This kind dog had helped a lost woman understand that it's not the outside package that makes people valuable; it's the truth, the hope, and the new heart that beats within them. All these things she had found in the loving arms of God.

Laurie sat in the darkened closet and cried. She hoped that Mia would be calmed by the soft, rhythmic strokes of her master's hand over the top of her head. In the lowest of tones, Laurie sang songs that had always filled her aching heart with comfort. She sang songs to God, songs that promised peace for her struggling girl. Bending down, Laurie moved her lips close to her dying dog's ear, making sure Mia heard her every word.

My precious girl, you're the best dog in the world.

"My precious girl, you're the best dog in the world. Sweet baby, I love you."

Laurie watched as Mia slipped into a peaceful sleep. She cupped Mia's face with both hands and offered one final prayer, knowing this would be their last moment together.

"Thank you, God, for allowing me to know Mia and for

blessing my life by letting me take care of her during our short time as a family. Thank you, Lord, for showing me a deeper glimpse of who you are through this little blind dog… Thank you…thank you."

The murmured words mixed with her silent tears. When Laurie finished praying, she bent down even farther and gently, repeatedly kissed Mia's nose and muzzle. Finally she pressed her wet cheek against Mia's face and just held her.

"I love you, Mia. I love you, sweet girl. You will always be my precious girl… I love you." Laurie wanted a message of loving adoration to be the last thing Mia heard.

Laurie slipped out of the closet and into her bed. She cried long into the darkness, mournful sobs of anguish and grief. Her friend was dying. She tried to console her breaking heart by focusing on the fact that, for the last several months, Mia had been greatly loved. She wouldn't die alone under a bush or an old car. Laurie reminded herself that Mia was cradled in a warm, safe place with the one person who loved her, and now she was in a deep, tranquil sleep. Laurie wept until she had no more tears.

Morning came too soon, with the light from Laurie's bedroom window still flat and gray. The radiant warmth of the sun had not yet reached into her world of sorrow. In the silence of the early dawn, Laurie lay motionless, emptied and exhausted, trying to comprehend all that had happened.

Did I do it right, God? Did I look after her enough? Did she know how much she was loved?

Finally, the light in her window began to glow with the golden promise of a new day. There would always be a new day. Laurie prayed out of her aching heart. "Oh, God, I need your help. I don't know how to do this. I don't know how to push through this grief."

Laurie rolled to the side of her bed—and froze. Her eyes remained fixed on the floor, stunned by the sight. Apparently, at some point during the night, Mia had rallied long enough to relocate herself, as close to Laurie as she could get. She lay curled up on the floor, only inches away from the bed.

"Oh, Mia... My precious Mia," Laurie whispered.

It took a moment before she could muster the will to touch her. Finally, leaning over to stroke her beloved dog one last time, Laurie touched Mia's head. She was surprised by a hint of warmth.

"Oh, God." She spoke aloud to him. "If only I'd known earlier that she was here, I could've held her as she died." The fact that Laurie had missed Mia's passage by moments wounded her heart even deeper.

She touched Mia again.

Under her hand, she felt a twitch, ever so slight.

What's happening? She jerked her hand away and stared at her dog.

With resolve, Laurie reached down and placed her hand on Mia's smooth head. As if in slow motion, she moved her hand down her dog's body. Suddenly, Mia lifted her head and looked up at her.

What? Mia was alive—very much alive!

Incredulous, Laurie looked down at her revived dog. Her thoughts collided with an instant logjam of questions. *How can this be?* Her bewilderment was interrupted by the familiar *thump, thump, thump* of Mia's tail drumming against the carpet. It was the most welcome sound Laurie had ever heard. Mia peered up at her master as if to ask, "Hey, what's for breakfast?"

Laurie slid out of bed and onto the floor beside her dog. She wrapped Mia in her arms and pulled her close. Laurie buried her face into her dog's neck, crying and laughing at the same time.

"Thank you, God! Thank you, God! Thank you, God!" poured like a river out of her heart, flooding her soul with gratitude.

In that moment, Laurie's mind reeled backward through

every random conversation concerning Mia. Conversations that discussed the dog that some thought wasn't worth saving.

"She's too messed up."

"She has too many problems."

"Just leave her. Let her go."

The comments reverberated in her head, while the parallels to her own life resounded even louder. God hadn't given up on her when she looked too far-gone to save. When others left her for dead because they believed she was too messed up, the Lord stayed with her. Unlike her accusers, he didn't focus on all her failures. Neither did he ask her to clean up her life before coming to him. Instead, when she cried out his name, he came to her.

Without judgment, the Lord of all had crawled into her darkest closet, and instead of criticizing her, he cradled her. He focused not on what she lacked but on who she was. He didn't consider her faults; he only saw her potential.

Even though she had committed many offenses, he spoke of none. Out of his mouth did not pour the expected reprimands. From his lips flowed only his truth. Of all the things he could have said in her most broken states, he didn't. The only words that poured from his heart into hers were how perfectly he created her, how deeply he believed in her, and how completely he loved her.

Laurie embraced her dog in the midst of Mia's eager good morning kisses and was blanketed by more truth.

Even though Laurie had felt all alone the night before, God had not abandoned her. During her bleakest and most abysmal moments, God had always been by her side. In all those places and times when she lay in the darkness, so broken and heavy-hearted that she felt she might be crushed by the blackness, God had been with her.

Deep in the caverns of her soul, in the times when her spirit felt closest to death, that was when she had heard it—the voice of Jesus.

And he was praying for her, speaking words of love over her. Words of peace. Words of truth. Words of comfort.

And then—hope beyond hope—she could hear something else, the most beautiful melody to ever fill her soul.

It was her Lord…singing…over *her*.

The LORD your God is with you,
> he is mighty to save.
> He will take great delight in you,
> he will quiet you with his love,
> he will rejoice over you with singing.[2]

15

The Hope

Like a pair of compass needles pointing north, our horses traversed the last of the trail leading back to the ranch. Grateful for their autopilot ability, I pulled up the corduroy collar of my coat and used it to wipe away my tears. I looked across at my friend and exhaled, releasing the remnants of all that I had been holding in while she told about that night with Mia. The reins were draped over Lightfoot's neck while Laurie cupped her face with both hands.

I watched my friend. Without a doubt, her tears were shed from a recently forged gratitude deep within her heart. They flowed from a woman who was being refined. These were tears that fell from a new place, a new start of freedom. They were not a release of sorrow, but a sweet herald of joy.

Laurie looked up and smiled through her tears. "No one ever warned me that when you rescue a dog, the life you save just might be your own!"

She wiped her tears. "In crazy and surprising ways, God has a much greater purpose for this exceptional dog to be in my life. I have chosen to receive this extra time with my beloved girl as a windfall from him, a priceless gift. Because of our unexpected second chance, Mia and I will continue our journey together down this remarkable road. Apparently I still have more to learn from her...much more."

When you rescue a dog, the life you save just might be your own!

"I do too," I said. "I don't think Mia's done with me either!"

"Yes, it will take me a lifetime to apply the truths she has modeled. For years I tried to build my life on sand by attempting to gain value, acceptance, and love from places, activities, and people. But my blind dog led me to the Rock, Jesus Christ, and helped me to see that he is the only firm foundation.

"Even though I tried to satisfy my heart with everything but him, his love for me never faltered. No matter how far I ran away from him, he never strayed from me. Through all of my wandering and wayward times, he remained beside me and offered his love, hope, and peace. Yet his gifts became effective in my life only when I finally stopped being my own master and started trusting him."

Laurie told me about the many times when she and Mia went for walks, only to have Mia experience an insulin crash. At first this irritated Laurie because she couldn't finish her jog or walk. But over time, Laurie's focus shifted from herself to Mia. Her dog was sick and needed her help. From then on, whenever Mia showed signs of crashing, Laurie turned around without hesitation and headed toward their house or car. Nearly every time this happened, Mia would not be able to make it back on her own. That was when Laurie would kneel down, lift Mia to her chest, and carry her home.

"It was during one of those episodes that God reminded me how he has done the exact same thing for me. Of all the times in my life when I couldn't go on in my own strength, my Lord was there to pick me up and carry me. I now understand that God will always carry me home."

Laurie shifted in her saddle. "Mia taught me that blind hope doesn't grope around in the darkness trying to find the way. Blind hope doesn't depend on what it can feel. Blind hope depends on what it knows! Authentic hope depends on what is true. Hope that is real doesn't come from what we can see—it comes from our heart, from the inside out. It comes from Christ alone."

As if in agreement with Laurie's words, a billowing gust of wind swirled around us. Strands of black hair pulled free of my riding helmet and whipped around my face. I looked at Laurie and nodded.

She tucked a few flaxen wisps of hair back under her helmet. "Through a forsaken, blind Aussie dog, God has shown me what genuine love and hope actually look like. Mia reflected my own impoverished state and then provided me with the best example, her own life, to reveal just how much my Master loves me."

We rode the horses under the sturdy wooden beams of the main gate, up the hill, and into the common yard. Ele and Lightfoot, with fourteen years of trail riding under their saddles, turned like magnets toward the hitching rail. I eased my mare's gear off and started toward the tack room. Laurie met me with a saddle balanced over her arm.

We walked shoulder to shoulder across the wood chip–covered yard. I couldn't resist checking in with my friends, so I glanced over at the peaks in the Cascade Range.

My dog was blind…but now I see.

Bathed in glorious streams of sunlight, they beamed back, appearing to shimmer their majestic appreciation of all that had just happened in our lives. Not wishing to walk past the moment, we stopped and received the alpine approval. Laurie turned to me, her face a glowing reflection of the radiance that lay before us.

"It's true. For the rest of my life, I'll be grateful for this fact: my dog was blind…but now *I* see."

Epilogue

Like the rising of the sun, hope streams forth. Its radiance banishes dark despair in the hearts of those who receive it. Hope summons us to stretch, to step forward, to reach higher than ourselves. Hope transforms all who embrace it.

What a wonder it has been to watch this renewal of hope in the life of my friend. Day by day, choice by choice, Laurie has persevered to leave her anxiety and pride behind. In their place, peace and gentleness have grown. Where a vacant life of selfishness once echoed with a lonely voice, a life brimming with authentic love now reverberates with satisfaction.

Laurie would be the first to proclaim that she's methodically working through her flaws and hasn't attained anything admirable thus far. However, as her friend, I politely disagree.

It is not her words but her actions that reflect the changes inside her heart. Laurie is submitting her life to God. With his help, she is exchanging her despair for his joy, her fear for his peace, her anger for his love.

Her life is not perfect, but it is peaceful.

Out of this new abundance, Laurie pours out to others all that has been poured into her. She not only works at Crystal Peaks Youth Ranch, but since following God's design revealed through a little blind dog, Laurie has been promoted to team leader. One of the roles of a team leader is to motivate others through encouragement and example. Laurie has volunteered to oversee and co-lead a group called SAGE (Seeking After God Entirely), which mentors teenage girls who visit the ranch.

Remember that marathon we trained for? Laurie and I ran it together stride for stride. We crossed the finish line with hands joined, our arms raised together in united triumph.

Mia, although slowing down, continues to place one steadfast paw in front of the other, moving forward with her master. The once unwanted dog in need of rescue remains loyal to Laurie, staying true to the task of loving the woman she rescued.

As for me, I still believe I'm the most blessed woman on earth. I'm privileged to live in proximity to kids, horses, volunteers, and my family of staff. I cry and laugh with them and cheer them on. In every way, I'm sharpened and filled by them.

As if that weren't enough to fill my life with gratitude, every night I walk up the hill and fall into the arms of a husband who loves me.

Like other rescue stories on the ranch, Laurie and Mia's reveals how something beautiful happens when we're selfless in our actions. In our efforts to reach out and save another in need, our own heart is often released from selfishness, isolation, and defeat. In a world weakened by loneliness, great strengthening can happen if we choose to reach beyond our own difficulties and do something for the benefit of someone who is hurting.

Although our society is highly motivated to recycle things like paper and plastic, we are too often quick to discard damaged people and abandoned animals. With minimal effort, each of us can find the forsaken and rejected souls within our midst. Volunteering opportunities abound, whether it's mentoring a child, supporting a rescue facility, or adopting an animal. Each of us can make a difference. We can

> *In a world weakened by loneliness, great strengthening can happen if we choose to reach beyond our own difficulties and do something for the benefit of someone who is hurting.*

all stand in the gap for those around us who are struggling to find their way.

The truth is, in the greater picture, we're all struggling to find our way. Similar to Laurie's dog, none of us can see what lies ahead. Like Mia, you might be bounding forward in defiance, circling in panic, or trotting along at your Master's heels. Maybe you're curled up in a dark place, too weak to crawl out of your devastation. Wherever you are in this life, whatever challenges you might face, however hopeless your situation appears, there is help.

Friend, we have a rescuer.... His name is Jesus.

No matter what our stage of life, we can always turn toward our Master. Because of Jesus and his great love, regardless of where our choices have led us, we can always choose to turn around. We can always choose him. And when we do, he will come...he will pick us up...and he will carry us home.

What can we say about such wonderful things as these?
If God is for us, who can ever be against us?[3]

I am convinced that nothing can ever separate us
from his love. Death can't, and life can't. The angels
can't, and the demons can't. Our fears for today, our
worries about tomorrow, and even the powers of hell
can't keep God's love away. Whether we are high above

the sky or in the deepest ocean, nothing in all creation will ever be able to separate us from the love of God that is revealed in Christ Jesus our Lord.[4]

For if you confess with your mouth that Jesus is Lord and believe in your heart that God raised him from the dead, you will be saved. For it is believing in your heart that you are made right with God, and it is by confessing with your mouth that you are saved.... "Anyone who calls on the name of the Lord will be saved."[5]

Acknowledgments

I'm grateful for

- Brian Thomasson, who cried when I first shared the idea of this story.
- Joel Kneedler, who encouraged me to write this book.
- Alice Crider, who loves animals as much as I do.
- Judy Gordon Morrow, who shouldered with me to do the impossible—again.
- Jenni Reiling, Judy Jeffery, and Larry and Katie Kepple, who prayed this project to life.
- the staff at Crystal Peaks Youth Ranch, who combined all their efforts to clear a time path for me.
- Troy Meeder, who is the love of my life.
- Jesus Christ, who is my life.

Notes

1. See Isaiah 6:2–3.
2. Zephaniah 3:17, NIV.
3. Romans 8:31.
4. Romans 8:38–39.
5. Romans 10:9–10, 13.

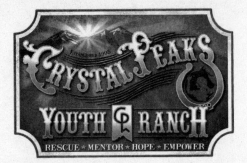

OUR MISSION

Crystal Peaks Youth Ranch was founded in 1995 by Troy and Kim Meeder.

After the rescue of its first two abused horses, something wonderful and unexpected happened; children began to come to the ranch. In their simple but passionate efforts to help the horses, they themselves embraced emotional healing. By what can only be attributed to the compassion of a loving God, the lives of the children and horses began to change.

Since the inception of the Ranch, abuse, loneliness and sorrow have been replaced with peace, belonging and joy. It is a healthy, faith-based environment where children, families and horses choose to embrace hope within the healing circle of unconditional love and support.

Crystal Peaks Youth Ranch exists to
RESCUE the horse,
MENTOR the child,
offer HOPE for the family
and EMPOWER the ministry.

Please visit our website to:

- Learn about our programs
- Sign up to participate in information clinics
- Find similar ministries in your area
- Find out how you can share hope

www.crystalpeaksyouthranch.org

We would be happy to hear from you.
E-mail us at blindhope@cpyr.org.

STORIES FROM THE RANCH OF RESCUED DREAMS

Follow a horse where no one else can tread, through the minefield of pain that surrounds a broken child's soul. From a mistreated horse to an emotionally starved child and back again, a torrent of love revives their barren places.

In the presence of unconditional love, a mute girl speaks for the first time. A defiant teenager teaches a horse to trust again...and opens his own heart to love. A rescued horse gives a dying man his last wish. A battered girl finds love and protection in the friendship of a battered horse.

Come visit a place where the impossible flourishes, where dreams survive the inferno of reality—a place where hope rises.

SOMETIMES, JUST BELIEVING IN SOMEONE IS ENOUGH FOR THEM TO START BELIEVING IN THEMSELVES...

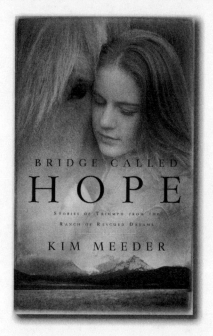

Hope is like the stars—always there, yet shining brightest in the blackest of nights. It is like the dawn, always rising anew. Hope is for everyone. This collection of more than twenty true stories from the ranch of rescued dreams unveils the heart of true strength and the character of genuine courage. Experience the kind of love and hope that can change a person from the inside out. Because sometimes, just believing in someone is enough for them to start believing in themselves. It's the galvanizing truth that no matter how deep your pain...God's love for you is deeper still.